MR. SNOW'S GUIDE TO WINNIING LAWSUITS

Seven Steps to Legal Victory

William Snow
Author and Entrepreneur

Mr. Snow's Guide to Winning Lawsuits
www.winninglawsuitguide.com

Publisher
10-10-10 Publishing
Markham, ON
Canada

Printed in Canada and the United States of America

Contents

DEDICATION

This book is dedicated to my wonderful son, who has always been, and will always be, my reason to push forward.

FOREWORD

If you are involved in a civil lawsuit, either as plaintiff or defendant, it is up to you to present all necessary information to your attorney and the Court in order to successfully argue your case. A civil lawsuit can be a very complex and difficult undertaking. If you do not understand the court system and the legal process you could be heading for a lot of unnecessary hardship and anguish.

This is why I am so excited about this book, *Mr. Snow's Guide to Winning Lawsuits.* William Snow has come up with a seven step plan to help you navigate through what can be a very difficult process. He is sincere and honest, and displays through personal stories the obstacles that may be present if you are involved in a civil lawsuit. William Snow shows you how important it is to plan ahead and evaluate your situation before starting a lawsuit, and how to protect yourself successfully if you are served with one. The importance of choosing the right attorney can not be over-emphasized, and understanding the courtroom atmosphere and procedures are vital for you to be successful when involved in a civil lawsuit. William Snow discusses these topics in depth.

The fact that you are holding this book right now indicates that you may be thinking about filing a lawsuit, or may be involved in one. The preparation for your case and the knowledge of the legal system can and will affect the outcome of your case, and the decision that the Court ultimately makes.

Although William Snow is not an attorney, he demonstrates a great deal of knowledge of the legal system, and helps prepare you for a civil lawsuit on a layperson's terms. He has found a way to keep you engaged, while reading through a complex and difficult topic. Though he is discussing U.S. law, his practical and personal examples make the process much easier for you to understand. His friendly and professional tone will win you over, and his demonstrated acumen on the subject will impress you.

It is clear that civil lawsuits are an area of passion for Mr. Snow, and he clearly does not want anybody taken advantage of or misled. His passion is contagious. I can feel his joy at times, and his pain at others, when he writes about his own personal experiences in this book. I believe you will be inspired to make significant changes in your approach to a civil lawsuit after reading this book.

If you are involved in a civil lawsuit, *Mr. Snow's Guide to Winning Lawsuits* is the book for you. If you have ever felt slighted by your end results from a past lawsuit, reading this book will explain why. After reading this book, you will have a new understanding of the legal system, the difficulties that can arise when involved in a civil lawsuit, and how to proceed and prepare for the future if you find yourself involved in one.

Raymond Aaron
New York Times Bestselling Author

ACKNOWLEDGMENTS

I was extremely blessed to have the support and guidance of many wonderful people, to whom I want to express my sincere gratitude:

To my wonderful son, Dad loves you.

To Raymond Aaron, for his words of wisdom, his support, and his genuineness for helping others.

To Cara Witvoet, my book architect, for her helpful insight and positive attitude throughout this entire project.

To my amazing friend, Alicia Couri, who held me accountable to finish this book.

To my good friends, Jesse Baker and Naomi Castillo, who encouraged me to write and finish this book.

To my dear friends, Judge Arlene Gordon-Oliver and Dr. Prabash Koneru.

To the individuals who have, in their own special way, supported me throughout the creation of this book: Chris O'Hara, Qaiser Afridi, Benjamin Schwartz, Okema Royes, and of course, my dogs, both of which took turns sitting on my lap while I was writing this book.

I would also like to thank all of those people who caused the legal controversies in my life, and/or misrepresented me legally, without whom I would not have been able to write this book so accurately in order to educate others.

x

WHY THIS BOOK

President Donald Trump has been involved in lawsuits. Hillary Clinton has been involved in lawsuits. Many famous people have been involved in lawsuits. However, one doesn't have to be famous to get sued, or sue somebody, in this country. Anybody can sue anybody, and be involved in a lawsuit. The odds are that someday, in one's lifetime, he or she will be involved in a lawsuit.

Per the common good, 80% of all lawyers in the world live in the United States. The American Bar Association reports there are more lawyers per capita in the United States than in any other country. According to the State Court Guide to Statistical Reporting, over 15 million civil lawsuits are filed per year in the United States. The *Economic Journal* writes that Americans spend twice as much on civil litigation than they do on their new cars—and we Americans love our cars.

The question is: why is this so? The answer is: it is easy to sue people in this country. Lawsuits are made available to the public, and people are usually not punished for starting frivolous lawsuits. With so many lawyers available in the United States, it becomes easy for one to find a lawyer who will take their case to sue somebody. Lawyers are looking for work. Lawsuits keep them in business. Lawyers are everywhere. Advertisements for personal injury attorneys can be seen on billboards and television, and heard on radios. Simply dial a number to start a lawsuit. People see it as a get-rich-quick scheme. Perhaps some lawsuits are, but a major lawsuit can be very painful and life changing. It is one thing to sue, which can actually backfire, and it is another thing to get sued.

A common, expensive civil lawsuit in this country is divorce and custody of children. With over 60% of marriages ending in divorce, family law and divorce court is big business. Divorce and custody battles can continue for years, and can be extremely expensive and costly. They can run into the millions of dollars. Civil litigation can also last years, and can cost millions of dollars, depending on the parties involved.

Since litigation is big business in this country, the odds are that it will never end or be regulated in any way. So, therefore, the real question to ask is, "If I am involved in a lawsuit, can I win?"

That is a good question: can I win? This will involve many factors, not all of which you have control over. As a legal client, you do not have control over a lot of things. In fact, the lawsuit itself may cause you a lot of hardship.

My pen name is William Snow, and I am writing this book because I have been involved in several lawsuits—sometimes winning and, at other times, losing—whether I deserved to or not. I am not using my real name or indicating where I live; I want to write this book accurately, and I do not want litigious people from my past suing me. I've had enough of that. I feel I could not write this book accurately and effectively with the potential threat of a lawsuit, and I want people to know what the legal system can really be like. I am writing this book for potential defendants of lawsuits, and for possible plaintiffs too. I was not trained as a lawyer but, in fact, was trained in a completely different field. I write this book to educate the layperson on what they are getting themselves into when they involve themselves with the legal system, and to guide them on winning their case as best as they can. I say *"as best as they can"* because it seems that no client, with few exceptions, truly wins a lawsuit. This is not a get-rich- quick book through the legal system, and anyone who tells you that the legal system can be used for that purpose is, at the least, unethical and, at the most, a fraud after your money.

I am writing this book as someone who has been a legal client for over ten years. I was sued four times. Three times were major lawsuits, including a divorce and custody battle. Another lawsuit I was involved in included a place I worked in, having to do with a dispute between an administrator and myself. A third lawsuit involved a contractor suing me for work he had not completed on real estate I owned, and he was trying to get more money out of me. My legal problems have involved businessmen and an ex-spouse, which makes me very knowledgeable on civil lawsuits. I was sued a fourth time by a neighbor of a property I owned because a tenant of mine built a bicycle ramp too near a neighbor's rickety old fence, and I had to appear on a television court show to defend myself.

In all of these cases, I actually did win something; except I lost on the television court show, which paid the plaintiff $500, although I, and others, thought it was ridiculous. I paid nothing, and friends and colleagues of mine were able to spend the day at a television studio, and appear on television, which was a lot of fun.

As far as winning lawsuits, I did win a lawsuit when I was involved in an automobile accident in a southern state, on my way to work. A person driving a Cadillac drove right through a red light and plowed into me, totaling my Honda. I went to the hospital, had x-rays and a CT scan done, and went for physical therapy for a number of months. I had hired a lawyer off of a big billboard in the city I lived in at the time, and ended up with a whopping $1200, after months of physical therapy.

However, I have also taken two of my former attorneys to the Bar Counsel: I won $16,000 from one of them, and $30,000 from another, who messed up my case against the administrator. This attorney ended up paying for the whole lawsuit—not me.

As far as the divorce and custody battle, I ended up with custody of my son, after having lost custody because of an act committed by a former attorney. After firing him, and finally finding a good attorney, my son came to live with me, and has been living with me ever since.

As far as the real estate lawsuit, the contractor received about $12,000, and this was after he thought he had taken advantage of me with multiple real estate deals. At the time, it appeared that I had lost a significant amount of money. However, it is real estate—even if you mess up, it can still pay off over time through depreciation and rental income. I made well over ten times the amount I invested in the properties, and certainly a lot more than the contractor made. Well, the Universe does have a way of rewarding those who deserve it. I was actually able to live off of those properties for a number of years.

So, I guess I do know how to win, whether I am being sued or suing. Over the years, I have worked with a total of fourteen attorneys, with my present attorney being the best one I ever retained. Comparing him with the others allows me to share what I have learned about attorneys over the years.

I have also been up against at least eight attorneys, and have learned a great deal from them, especially by being cross examined by them. I know many of their techniques, and can pass them onto you.   I have been trained by previous attorneys on how to testify properly, whether in depositions or in court, and I will cover this. I have been through two full trials, and I have experienced what it is like for a judge to make a decision. I recommend this be avoided since, when a judge makes a decision, it becomes a crapshoot, and all control is lost. I have been in front of at least six judges, some of who were brilliant, with the most incredible minds to learn from, and others who were a disaster and should not be behind the bench.

I have experience working with expert witnesses, including medical experts, psychologists, forensic accountants, guardian ad litems, and law guardians, all of which need to be paid for by you.

I am more than aware of the expenses incurred in a lawsuit, and to whom they have to pay (many of which the client has to pay). Legal expenses include paperwork fees (such as your attorney writing up complaints), answering complaints, processing server fees, court filing fees, telephone calls between you and your attorney, and between your attorney and opposing counsel, expert witness fees, and travel fees, to name just a few.

With all the experience and knowledge I have gained from my lawsuits, I now give to you my seven steps to winning a lawsuit.

CHAPTER 1

Step 1: Define What Winning is to You

Everyone wants to win. It always makes us feel good when we win. When we win, we feel happy and satisfied. So, how does one win a lawsuit? I guess one wins if they feel happy and satisfied when it is over. Therefore, one has to decide what outcome will make them happy and satisfied. A lawsuit involves preparation and strategy, and does pit one side against the other. Some may look at it as a competition. Although not a civil suit, anybody who watched the OJ Simpson trial could have felt that it was a competition, and OJ selected his dream team of attorneys.

However, a lawsuit is not like a football game, where you score more runs or points than the other team. It is more like a boxing match, where you have to convince judges that you presented a more convincing fight, or case, than the other side. Just like a boxing match, a lawsuit is never a sure thing. Many boxing matches have been decided by judges who choose the apparent losing boxer. This can happen in court also. Don't let anyone tell you that it is a sure thing. Nobody wants to hand over large sums of money or property, and people will fight, and fight hard, to keep what they own or possess.

This first step in defining what winning is will be crucial. If you want to sue somebody, then you must look at the lawsuit as an investment. It will involve time and money. Winning for you may be to not start the lawsuit at all. This is something you will have to discuss with your attorney. For example, recently I worked with a group of people who clearly owed me a large sum of money. I appeared to have a fairly good lawsuit. The only issue was that it would have to be litigated in a state far from where I live, and my attorney was not willing to litigate in that state, unless the other party sued me first.

Due to my knowledge of lawsuits, and the fact that I could not use the attorney I wanted to use, I decided not to go ahead with the lawsuit. The risk of using an unknown attorney, and litigating in a foreign jurisdiction, outweighed my desire to go after the money that I felt was owed me. I realized, in this case, there were easier ways to make money, and that it was not worth it. This is a point that I really want to emphasize. Winning a lawsuit may be to **not start the lawsuit at all.** You need to look at the lawsuit as an investment.

If you decide to go ahead with the lawsuit, and if it is money that you want, then decide how much money you want, and if it is worth pursuing. If you were injured in an accident, and have a physical injury that is documented with medical testing or imaging, and the injury is clearly affecting the way you live your life, then the lawsuit is most likely worth pursuing. You should be compensated for the injury you sustained if it was due to someone else's negligence or intent. The amount that you should ask for will be discussed with your attorney. If the lawsuit does not include a physical injury, it may not be as clear as to whether you will win or not.

In the potential lawsuit that I described above, I decided not to go ahead with it. It could potentially be worth $96,000 to me, based on a vague agreement that was signed, and there was a breach committed. However, the other side did have legitimate arguments also. Now, $96,000 is a lot of money, and many people who are unfamiliar with the legal system may have gone for it. Given the circumstances and parties involved, and after a long discussion with my attorney, I decided not to go ahead with it. It was not a sure thing, and the numbers were not big enough. If it was $960,000, then I may have decided differently; or, maybe, I still would not have pursued it, due to other factors, like whether the opposing party would be able to pay that amount or not.

That is an important consideration when deciding what winning is to you. If it is money that you are after, it pays to sue somebody with deep pockets, such as an insurance company. If you sue a person or small business, they may not have the money to pay, and you will never see it.

Perhaps it is property that you are after; once again, you need to decide what winning is to you. I have seen divorce cases where people fight over a lamp. They can spend thousands of dollars on their legal fees to pursue a lamp worth $250. If you win the lamp, was it worth it? Perhaps you are fighting over real estate, such as a house. Then perhaps winning the title of the house, or the right to live in the house, is what you consider winning.

When I think of my lawsuits, I had to decide what winning was. For my child custody battle, it was easy to define. At first, I wanted joint legal custody of my son, and I wanted very liberal visitation. I also did not want my son to relocate to another state. That was a very hard-fought battle, where I obtained joint legal custody of my son, but my visitation was not what I wanted and, eventually, he was able to relocate with his mother. I felt I lost that battle. My ex-wife was asking for a significant amount of money from my future earnings. She did not receive that, so I felt I won that battle. Years later, when my son was much older, I wanted full custody of him, as well as the ability to relocate him back to living with me. I did win that. With law, if one loses at first, they can win later on, if persistent enough. In this case, winning was clearly defined. In addition, this also demonstrates that what one defines as winning may change over time and circumstances.

In the lawsuit with my place of employment, at first, my idea of winning was to countersue the institution and the CEO, and win a substantial amount of money for defamation of character. However, my first two attorneys were running up such a large legal bill that, after a while, I just wanted to survive the lawsuit, and end it with as little damage as possible. I switched attorneys, and my second attorney filed a proceeding wrong, and the judge ended up awarding my opposition $10,000. At that time, I felt like I was getting my butt kicked, and I did not know what to do. The CEO of the institution still wanted to pursue me for his own personal reasons. Luck had it that I found another attorney who filed a motion against the institution and against the institution's attorneys. In a week and a half, the institution settled and agreed that I pay the $10,000 that the judge had awarded them, and the case was over. I lost the $10,000, but I ended the case, so I both lost and won. I ended up taking my former attorney, who filed the proceedings wrong, to Bar Council, and I was awarded back the $10,000, plus legal fees I had paid him for his negligence. He is still paying me back monthly. So, in the end, my former attorney paid the institution, and I did not lose any money.

This is a good point to bring up. Sometimes winning is stopping a lawsuit that was filed against you. In that case, you did not file it. Ending a lawsuit filed against you will stop a lot of mental and emotional hardship, and can save you a lot of time and money. Many times, when a lawsuit ends, it makes you feel happy and satisfied, depending on the situation. With my lawsuit against the institution I worked at, I felt temporary relief when the lawsuit ended. However, I still felt cheated and violated by what had been done to me, and by whom. I felt that way a long time, until the CEO of the institution was fired and escorted out of the institution, and was told never to return to the premises. That made me feel better, although it had not taken place in the courtroom. Winning can happen out of the courtroom; and remember, karma can be a bitch, and can eventually bite you in the ass.

In a lawsuit, when you end up in court, and the two sides cannot come to an agreement, winning may go out the window, and the judge may not award you what you feel you deserve. The judge is not going to necessarily agree with you. Although a small case, the case I had on television was absurd. I did not know the neighbor who claimed my tenant had destroyed his fence. When I looked at the fence, it was a filthy, cheap, old fence, and the owner had sued me without even complaining to me about it. He apparently just wanted money and his 15 minutes of fame that Andy Warhol promised him on television. He really had no case, and the judge came up with my being responsible for a nuisance, and awarded him $500, which was $300 less than he had asked for. The judge also commented that it appeared to be a very inexpensive fence. I disagreed with the ruling, as others, who watched the case, did as well. Be that as it may, anything can happen in the courtroom when the judge, or a third party, is making the decision.

In the case against the institution, the judge felt that I should pay the institution $10,000 for the error my lawyer had made. Bar Counsel felt I deserved to be paid by my former lawyer for the error he had made. A lot depends on the context of what is being presented, and who is deciding the case. The main point is that winning is a lot harder to decide once a third party is making a decision, and you lose control of the case.

A divorce and custody battle is usually a situation where nobody wins, except the attorneys. The only winning occurs when it ends, and the parties can lick their wounds. This is one situation where it is best for all parties involved to stay out of court and resolve it by settling. Since neither side really wins, no matter what the outcome, the lawyers want to keep the fighting going as long as possible, since they make their money through legal hours. **If you fight in a divorce case, the lawyers on both sides win, and cash in, and neither you nor your ex-spouse win anything.** I cannot emphasize this enough. There are some good divorce and family attorneys, but in my experience, your own attorney may be your worst enemy when it comes to divorce and custody. You need to be aware of this. Remember that everyone has their own agenda in this case, and it's not necessarily what is best for you, your ex-spouse, and your children.

With few exceptions, you really should approach the divorce as if your own attorney and the opposing side's attorney does not really care about your children. If you have that approach, then at least, for your children's sake, if you are both caring parents, then you won't continue to fight. Even if you win custody, the child still knows he/she has two parents, and if you use the child as a weapon, you may be shooting yourself in the leg. That same child you were fighting to keep away from the other parent can very well turn on you when he/she gets older, and then you have won nothing, and your lawyer took you to the bank.

Don't ever let your attorney tell you how to parent. They are attorneys—not experts on parenting. The advice they give you on parenting is not worth the money you paid them to hear it. I was on the phone with a former attorney one time, talking about my custody case with him, and his daughter started talking in the background. He started screaming and cursing at his 7-year-old daughter. He was known to be a good divorce and custody attorney. Do you really want somebody like that representing you and your children? This attorney was a horrible parent himself. The best way to win a custody battle is to do it out of court with a mediator. Do not give the attorneys the opportunity to capitalize on your anger for your ex-spouse, at the expense of your children. In my experience, the court does not care either, and much is decided by the judge's biases and prejudices. If you are going to fight and waste your money in a divorce, then do it over money or property. Just remember that the money you spent in legal fees could have been used for you and your children. It probably would have sent your children to college, instead of putting your attorney's children through college.

If you are in a car accident, or slip and fall somewhere and obtain an injury, then it will be a little more straightforward. There is an actual physical injury that can be shown and documented. It will also be necessary to show that the injury was caused by the car accident, fall, or incident, and that you had not suffered from the injury prior to the incident. The first thing you must do after an accident or a fall, is **not** leave the scene of the incident. If you do, the other side can argue that you were not really injured by the incident. Make sure an ambulance takes you away from the scene, and you are brought to an emergency room. You need to be examined at the emergency room and get evaluated. The doctor should be performing a history and physical exam. The doctor should also obtain lab tests, x-rays, Ct scans, MRIs, and whatever else is necessary for the workup of your injury.

Make sure everything is documented. Make sure there was a police report written also. Your attorney will need all of these records for your case. Your best bet in a personal injury case, at least from my experience and the experience of others, is to hire one of the personal injury attorneys who advertise and are on large billboards. They appear to know what they are doing. They are usually very experienced, and they know the doctors to send you to, and how to handle all of the court paperwork. For example, a friend of mine was in a car accident. He went to the hospital, had the workup done, and was found to have multiple injuries. He did not know who to call. I just started singing to him a song that two famous personal injury attorneys use in their advertising. He called them, and his case has been going very well. They have handled his case with expertise; he goes for physical therapy regularly, and will apparently receive a large judgment in his favor. He sustained real serious injuries that have affected his work, exercise, social life, and even his sex life.

I have heard of people faking these types of injuries, and I do not condone this. If you are faking it and get caught for fraud, you deserve it. I have heard of people, with alleged back injuries from accidents, going to the gym, staying out late and dancing, and even skydiving, after allegedly sustaining back injuries after an accident. Society does not have to, and should not have to, pay for fraud.

Many years ago, I was driving to work on a weekend. I was driving a Honda Accord. I was driving through an intersection, and a gentleman driving a Cadillac just plowed through the red light and hit me from the side. He essentially totaled my car. I was dazed and dizzy, but instead of going to the hospital, I called my ex-wife, who picked me up and drove me to my workplace after a police report was filled out. At the time, I was more concerned about being late for work than about the injuries I had sustained. As the day went on, I felt dizzier and dizzier. A friend of mine called me and told me that he heard I had been in an accident and that I had left the scene. He told me I should not have left the scene, and asked how I was feeling. I told him I was dizzy and my neck hurt a little. He instructed me to go to the emergency room immediately and to call an attorney. I did go to the ER, and I was evaluated and given a head CT and a CT scan of my neck. They instructed me to go home and rest.

In the city where I lived, there were large billboards plastered all over with the name and number of a well-known, personal injury attorney. I called them, and they told me to come into their office. They instructed me to see a doctor, and that I needed to discuss my case with the doctor, and that I may need treatment by a physical therapist for my injuries. I saw the doctors and had to go for six weeks of physical therapy. After all was said and done, I was awarded about $1200, and my car was repaired. I did learn some lessons from this. First, do not leave the scene of your incident. This is for health reasons, legal reasons, and financial reasons. I probably received less money than I should have for the accident and injuries I sustained. I was not aware of the extent of my injuries at first. The pain in my neck did not start until hours later, and the dizziness continued. You can be doing yourself a great disservice by just leaving the scene, even if you feel okay.

You also want to be brought to the hospital, on a stretcher, in an ambulance. If you can stand and walk away, then you probably are not, or do not appear, as injured or sick as you may be. In addition, the worse your injury is, the more compensation that you are likely to receive. In an injury lawsuit, there are many factors in deciding your monetary reward. This includes the severity of the injuries, whether the incident itself (e.g., car accident, fall) is responsible for your injury, and the effect the injury has on your lifestyle (causation). Your medical expenses are important, as well as your future medical expenses, if you have a good attorney. Do not forget to discuss medical expenses and future medical expenses with your attorney. Income lost from not being able to work is a factor, as well as any medical procedures that you need to endure, such as surgery or scans.

In summary, winning means different things to different people, and different situations. If you can define this early in your preparation process of a lawsuit, then you can save yourself hours of financial and emotional headache.

Review of Chapter

In this chapter, you learned Step 1 of winning a lawsuit. Winning is not the same for everybody—it depends on the situation. Before starting a lawsuit, decide what winning will be to you, and what you are willing to settle for.

If you are being sued, decide what winning is to you. As you will learn, when you are being sued, you can always countersue; so, winning may be ending the lawsuit so the plaintiff against you gets nothing, or winning the countersuit. Again, you have to decide what you will settle for.

In the next chapter, now that you have determined what winning is for you, it is time to determine what the risks are for you, and if winning is really worth it or not.

Notes

Notes

Notes

13

Notes

14

CHAPTER 2

Step 2: Define What the Risks Are

Before starting a lawsuit and suing somebody, you need to ask yourself, "What is the risk of suing somebody?" and, "Is the return or reward of the lawsuit worth the risk?" There are many risks to a lawsuit.

The first risk of suing somebody is that you may be sued yourself. The opposing party can countersue you. Whether they have a legitimate complaint or not, they can countersue you. In fact, this was a tactic my lawyer at the time used with my lawsuit against my place of employment. After the CEO and the institution had served me with papers starting their lawsuit, we answered the complaint with a countersuit against the institution and the CEO personally. Ultimately, that helped end the case. Now the defendant can become a counter plaintiff and ask for damages and monetary reward. So, the first risk of suing somebody is that you may be sued yourself. Be prepared for this. If you do not want to be sued yourself, or are not prepared for that, then don't start the lawsuit.

The second risk is that your lawsuit will go on public record. Unless the case is sealed, other people can find out about it. Do you want the general public to know your business? You could get a reputation of being litigious. You may or may not care about this. If you are a very private person, then you need to consider this. Court records are available for those who want to find them. This includes the media. The fact that you have sued people in the past can come up in future lawsuits, and gives the opposing counsel the opportunity to use this against you to say you are litigious, and that you like to file frivolous lawsuits. Again, depending on the circumstances, this may not matter to you.

The fact that the lawsuit is on public record presents the risk of your name appearing in the newspaper or media. There could be a story written about you, which may or may not be true. The media does not always report the truth—selling newspapers and getting high ratings are more important to them than your personal life or reputation. One of my lawyers decided to invite the press into the courtroom during my custody battle. He explained to me afterwards that this would be a good strategy since it would expose a group of dangerous people that were siding with my ex-wife. However, the reporter's story was distorted, and ended up costing me custody of my son at that time. I ended up firing my attorney and losing a lot of rights to my child. It was devastating to me.

A major issue with a lawsuit being on public record is that it can end up on the Internet. We now live in the Information Age, and legal records and news stories are readily accessible. Public exposure today is global and easy to locate. With the Internet, your name and lawsuit can be available for the world to see. It could affect your reputation. If you are a business owner, or work for an organization, do you want your name and lawsuit on the Internet for everyone to see? Do you want people reading details of your personal and professional life, on the Internet?   It can affect you professionally. It is possible to get the case impounded. This can prevent the public from seeing the case. It is something that you may want to discuss with your attorney

One of the tactics the institution used against me when they sued me was to put the lawsuit up on the Internet. The reporter published it on the Internet without ever speaking to me. It was a one-sided story, and it did hurt my reputation for a while, and that of others, outside the courtroom. It became difficult for me to find work. I applied for work at other places, and was going to receive employment, but my new potential employers quickly took back their offers of employment based on the false story they read on the Internet. Luckily, at that time, I was working for two other institutions. The administrators at both of those places eventually read the articles and questioned me about them. Nothing happened to me because both organizations were already familiar with my work, and they knew the reputation of the CEO who was suing me. Even though nothing happened, and both organizations renewed my contract, it was embarrassing explaining the situation to them.

On the other hand, being in the media could be helpful. Three other places, who also knew the reputation of the CEO that was suing me, hired me, and made me the director of a department for all three institutions. They knew the reputation of the CEO, and how he made it his hobby to fire and humiliate people publicly. Some of the administrators of the institutions had dealt with him before. In this case, I was hired because they admired the fact that I was not afraid to stand up to the CEO. They had learned about the lawsuit from the Internet. So, a risk could end up being a bonus in the long run, depending on what happens.

The next factor in deciding on starting a lawsuit is that it is going to take a lot of your time and energy. There are responsible people out there who may not have the time to pursue a lawsuit. There are also others who have no life to speak of, and lawsuits become their life. There are people who enjoy being litigious and making other people's lives miserable. I have experienced them many times.

A lawsuit requires a lot of time to prepare and carry out. It is not just your attorney putting in the time but you as well. The time spent preparing and litigating a lawsuit is going to take time away from other important issues in your life. You may have to miss work to meet with your attorney, or for depositions, or for appearing in court. The preparation for a lawsuit takes a lot of time.

Your attorney will want you to provide them with as much documentation as you have. This could require hours of time to find the paperwork, and to prepare it in reasonable order so your attorney can read and understand it. You may need to provide financial records, contracts, agreements, emails, medical records, and school records, depending on the case. You will have to spend the time locating these.

Trips to your attorney's office will take time, and will most likely occur during the workweek. There will be times when you will need to get papers notarized, and you will have to find a notary to do so. You will need to fax documents to your attorney, and there will be time needed to make copies and keep records.

In addition, you will need to answer your attorney's phone calls when he/she calls you. This can happen at any time of the day. This includes during work and when you may be in a meeting. You will most likely have to excuse yourself. The calls can come when you are with your family, and you really should answer them because you never know what they may be about. Many times, whenever I would see my attorney's number on my cell phone, my first reaction would be, "Oh shit, what now?" They usually call you for bad news rather than good, but that is not always true.

The biggest risk of all is the financial cost. A civil lawsuit can be very expensive. It will require money. As I said above, it will require time from you. It will also require time from your attorney, and you have to pay for that time. If you are defending yourself in a lawsuit, then you are losing from the start. I highly do not recommend representing yourself. You will have to pay a lawyer to defend you. No matter what the outcome you will have to spend money, time, and energy to defend yourself.

In defending yourself, your biggest risk could be your attorney. They will be charging you a retainer and billing you hourly. This includes phone calls, answers to complaints, hearings, motions, depositions, and a ton of paperwork and court appearances. Even if you choose to countersue, you will be charged by your attorney to write up the counterclaim. At times, the money being sucked out of your pocket is endless. The worst problem is when you get stuck with an unethical attorney who is trying to milk it for all its worth. Do not think that all attorneys are ethical and looking out for the best interests of their clients. You may get stuck with an ineffective attorney who is charging you a fortune and is incompetent.

My lawsuit with the institution demonstrates all of these risks. I was served with papers from one state while I was living in another. I had an attorney from the state I lived in, who I brought the papers to, since I did not have an attorney from the state in which I was being sued at the time. I had trusted the attorney from my home state at the time, which was a big mistake. He found me an attorney who was from the state of the lawsuit, and both were charging me money at the same time. The worst feeling is when one attorney is talking to the other, and you have to pay for both of them. You could be paying almost $1000 an hour for this. I can tell you now, from experience, that one great attorney is worth more than two or more attorneys who are not good. It is not necessary to have more than one attorney, and don't ever let them give you a false sense of security by telling you otherwise. Many times, they are double billing you for the same work.

The attorney, from the state from which the lawsuit was brought, went to a hearing and was able to prevent some of the institution's motions, but he ran up a bill of about $10,000 for one hearing, which was ridiculous. I was upset with the charges, and one of them said to me, "This is litigation; it's expensive." One can see how much of a rip off the legal system and attorneys can be. Then, a friend referred me to another attorney, who I later found out she had found on the Internet. I fired the other two attorneys and hired this one. He said he could handle the case, and that we should countersue, which neither of the other two attorneys had recommended—probably so they could keep billing.

I retained this new lawyer, and he took over the case and countersued. He first took a five thousand dollar retainer to review the case, and then requested another $25,000 to file a countersuit. However, he did not file his counter lawsuit properly, and it was done procedurally incorrectly. The judge threw out the counterclaim, and fined me $10,000. This new attorney had just made things much worse, and did not seem to care very much. He wanted to submit a new complaint. All the while, I was paying for his mistakes.

After this, I was devastated, and I found my current attorney by chance. In one week, he ended the whole lawsuit for $2000. He filed a motion with the court, and included personal information about the CEO. He pointed out how unethical he was, and also showed how his attorneys were trying to illegally manipulate the court venue. The case ended immediately, and the institution and CEO settled, with no fault on either side. I did have to pay the $10,000 my other attorney had lost me by incompetently filing his counterclaim.

What happened to me definitely illustrates the risks in a lawsuit. Besides the huge costs, there is a chance that you will hire an unethical attorney who will try to rob you blind, and double bill you, even if he is somewhat effective. You can get an incompetent attorney who will cost you a fortune, even if you have a great case like I did. There is the risk that your attorney will not use the right strategy, or will not know the right strategy to use. All of this will cost you time, money, and emotional hardship.

In addition, if you do have a bad attorney, and you have to switch attorneys, that will cost you more time and money. The new attorney will need to review the case and start fresh. This will all cost additional time and money. So, there are a lot of risks involved with a lawsuit.

When you are being sued, it can be even worse for you.

If you are suing somebody, or filing the complaint, it is best if you could find a lawyer who will take your case on contingency. Contingency means they will receive a percentage of the money that you are awarded or negotiated for in settlement. The percentage the attorney gets depends on what you negotiate with the attorney. Many times, it is 33%. There are also hybrid negotiations with attorneys, where you can pay a lower hourly rate, and also work on partial contingency. When the lawyer has to work on contingency, he/she has more incentive to perform well, since he/she will not get paid if he/she doesn't win. This takes away a lot of the risk from you. Unfortunately, if you are being sued, there is no contingency agreement available to you. If you file a countersuit, there may be, but you are still defending yourself from the original lawsuit, so any form of hybrid or contingency has to be worked out with your attorney.

There are also other unforeseen risks. This is especially true in the case of divorce. Divorce is a whole separate issue from other lawsuits. When it comes to divorce, some of the unforeseen risks are not seeing your children, losing your house, having your credit destroyed and, in severe cases, being admitted to a psychiatric ward—I have even observed suicide. I know a particular case where a father's ex-spouse would not let him see his daughters. He ended up in a psychiatric ward for over a month. There was another case where the mother's parents influenced the mother to not let the father see his children. Nobody could locate the father all weekend, and he was found dead, in a cabin in the woods, after having shot himself. There are ex-spouses and their relatives who care nothing about the children, and use the children as weapons. This is another great risk in a divorce suit. One final risk in a divorce is that one ex-spouse can claim that the other ex-spouse physically assaulted them or threatened them. This can lead to the arrest of one of the ex-spouses. Many times, these allegations are fictional, and there are unethical attorneys out there who will advise their client to have the other ex-spouse arrested. The attorney's trick is to have the ex-spouse arrested on a Friday, so they can't get out of jail until Monday, since the courts are closed.

There is another risk in a case, which has to be considered. That risk is the judge. There are many good judges out there who are brilliant people, and not only hear cases but decide the law of our land. Unfortunately, like in every other field, there are biased judges who do not belong behind the bench. In all fairness, this is not an easy job. Two sides of a story are presented to the judge, and they have to decide an outcome based on what is presented to them. There are times when it is not what is presented to them but how it is presented to them. Some lawyers happen to be better litigators than others, and can present cases better than another lawyer who is presenting the facts. There are judges who are completely biased or incompetent, and I have experienced them, and so have many others.

Without mentioning any particular judge, in Family Court, there does appear to be a lot of fathers complaining about the outcomes of their cases, and there have been father's rights groups formed, which have taken on a political cause. The odds are that these groups did not form because one or two fathers felt slighted. There are an awful lot of fathers who feel mistreated, especially when it comes to access to their children. Many of these fathers are decent parents who simply want to parent their child and, in my opinion, have just as much right as the mother to do so. What I have seen happen is, when the children are younger, they live with their mother, and as they become teenagers, many live with their fathers, by the children's own choice. I am not meaning to be political about this, but in the legal system, bias and prejudice does exist, which is another risk of lawsuits and litigation.

Now that winning, or the reward, was defined in the first chapter, and the risks were defined in this chapter, it is time to look at the risk/reward ratio in determining if the lawsuit is worth it. Look at the lawsuit as an investment. Take out a piece of paper and draw a line down the middle, from top to bottom. On the left side, list all the possible risks of the lawsuit, and on the right side, list all of the possible rewards. Take your time with this, and try to estimate the costs and benefits. Take another piece of paper, or perhaps use an excel spreadsheet, and figure out with numbers the real costs. The highest costs will be your attorney fees. However, there are other costs. If there are expert witnesses involved—such as forensic accountants, or forensic psychiatrists/psychologists—guess what; you have to pay for them. If you use multiple attorneys, you have to pay for them. You have to pay for filing fees and for process serving fees. Other costs you need to consider are travel, gas, parking, and loss of money from missing work; and there are the usually forgotten opportunity costs. These costs are what you could have been doing to earn money while you were spending your time on the lawsuit, or waiting around in court all day. While in court, you will be paying experts and your attorney by the hour, even if you have to wait six hours in the courtroom, before your case is even called. The odds are that you are **overestimating the benefits,** and **underestimating the costs**.

One nightmare that I went through was during my divorce. I had to sit in the courthouse while my attorney was telling the law guardian, or GAL (Guardian-ad-litem), dirty jokes. By the way, law guardians are supposed to represent the children. They have to be paid for, and you, as the party, pay for them. In my experience, they represent their wallets, and not the children at all. Again, divorce is a whole other matter. My point is, while my attorney was telling the law guardian his sexually inappropriate jokes, I was paying for both of them at the same time. The law guardian was female, and certainly was not offended by his sexist jokes since she was being paid $250 an hour to hear them. I just looked at the two of them, and snarled.

Review of Chapter

In this chapter, we learned that there are many risks in pursuing a lawsuit. This includes time, energy, and money, and some other possibilities, including arrest, admission to a psychiatric hospital, and possibly even death, if the pressure gets too heated.

When deciding whether or not to be involved in a lawsuit, you may sometimes not even have a choice; you need to analyze it as an investment, and do a risk/reward assessment or analysis, and you should write everything down.

If you decide that the reward is greater than the risk, and want to pursue the lawsuit, then you can advance to step 3 in the next chapter, which will determine your greatest cost and your greatest reward: finding a great attorney.

Notes

25

Notes

Notes

27

Notes

28

CHAPTER 3

Step 3: Find a Great Lawyer

This is probably the most important step. This will either make or break a lawsuit. The results will matter, depending on the attorney. In my experience, on the same case, one attorney cost me $10,000, and had my countersuit thrown out by the judge, while the other attorney, who took over the case, ended it in one and a half weeks, forcing the opposing side to give in. In the case of my custody battle for my son, one attorney cost me hundreds of thousands of dollars, and did virtually nothing for the case, while another attorney ended the case and got me custody of my son, as well as the ability to relocate him out of state, for $1500. It is amazing the difference in the outcomes, depending on the attorney. Unfortunately, this is your biggest risk, and could be your biggest reward.

How does one find a great attorney? That is a great question. How does one find a great doctor or accountant? The process is probably similar. First off, the attorney must be experienced in the type of case you are involved in. There are many different types of attorneys who specialize in different areas of law. For example, I would not hire a personal injury attorney to handle a child custody matter. A real estate attorney should not be handling a criminal case. Just like there are many different specialties for doctors, there are many different specialties for attorneys. Start by knowing what your case is. If you don't know what kind of case you have then ask an attorney you may know, what kind of case do I have? If you do not know an attorney you can ask about your case, then you can call the American Bar

Association and ask what kind of attorney they would recommend for your case after describing the case to them.

Many times it is just LUCK, as in my case. It was lucky that I was introduced to my current attorney, but I also recognized that he was a great attorney based on the poor attorneys I had prior. Essentially, it is luck that will get you a great attorney. However, I have learned that there are four types of luck, and each can cause you to end up with your attorney. The first type of luck is simply good luck. This is by chance. You actually end up with a decent attorney who is not trying to take advantage of you by overbilling you and ripping you off. There are many out there who really are good and decent.

The second type of luck is bad luck. This, too, is by chance. You may just end up with a lousy attorney. Since it took twelve lousy attorneys for me to find a great attorney, simply looking at the odds, if you go by pure chance, then the odds are you will get a lousy attorney. There appears to be more bad ones than good ones out there, by a large number.

The third type of luck involves doing research, listening, and developing good habits. This involves learning about the legal system and the different types of attorneys, and listening to the facts and advice I am giving in this book. This type of luck is not simply chance. It involves doing your homework, becoming aware of what is out there and what can happen, and acting on it when you see something wrong, or see something right. This is the best way to find a great attorney. This luck will protect you against a bad attorney, and will help you with a good attorney. I have heard that this kind of LUCK stands for **laboring under correct knowledge**. You need to jump on LUCK and be prepared for it.

The fourth type of luck is the opposite of the third. It is when you do the research, and get the right advice but ignore it, or you don't do the research at all. It is when you have been given good advice but don't follow it. This fourth type of luck can be very hazardous.

Now that you know there are many attorneys out there—some good, some bad, and many just downright ugly—there are many ways to locate an attorney. You can probably start by asking friends, relatives, colleagues, or coworkers if they know of any good attorneys. I did ask a friend for an attorney, and she did refer me to one. He started out great but became so nasty and opinionated, and was charging for things he should not have been charging for, so I fired him. So, even getting a referral does not always work. I once used my brother's attorney, and I would have been better off if I litigated the case myself. Even family referrals may not work. Perhaps a relative or friend of yours is an attorney, and can either represent you or lead you in the right direction. You can look up attorneys online. You can google attorneys. You can call the American Bar Association, and ask for attorneys in your area. There are many billboards and signs advertising attorneys. I did find a good one just by calling the number on a billboard. There are now legal membership clubs that can find you an attorney. What worked best for me was word of mouth but also knowing what to look for, and asking the right questions. I started using LUCK number three. Probably, the best way is to read this book, and at least have a checklist to ask your attorney. I have created one, which can be found at www.WinningLawsuitGuide.com.

The way I found my current and best attorney was by word of mouth, and by using LUCK number three. I was entering into a business deal with a colleague of mine. She told me her attorney would meet us at my office. She said he could handle our business venture. A young man walked into my office, and he kind of looked like a young boy at the time. He introduced himself as my friend's attorney, and I looked at him and felt I could not take him seriously. He did not look like the miserable, angry old white men or women that I had hired in the past. He started asking me about some of the cases I was Involved in with my other attorneys. He said they sounded like straightforward cases and should not have cost me that much. Of course, my angry old men attorneys had told me they were very complicated cases, and had been charging me a fortune. The more he talked, the angrier I became. After one week, I fired about five attorneys, and he took over all of my cases, in two states. He fixed up everything, with a minimal cost—one by one, my legal issues disappeared. I know what a great attorney is, since I have one.

So, based on my experience, what are the characteristics of a good attorney? Well, I had been to 12 attorneys before I found a good attorney; so, I pretty well can tell if an attorney is good or not. The first thing you should look for in an attorney is if he/she is acting professional. What I mean by *professional* is if he/she is on time for the appointment. Does he pay attention to you, and speak to you while you are in the office? Is he on the phone, taking care of other things, while you're sitting in the office? You can tell simply by the way he's acting towards you if this is a good attorney or not. If they are rude to you, just get rid of them.

Even if they have a great reputation, get rid of them if they don't treat you right. I had an attorney who was supposed to be one of the best real estate attorneys in the state, yet he was extremely obnoxious and nasty. I had even sent him and his law firm chocolates for Christmas. He called me and didn't even realize the answering machine was on. He was joking that I sent him chocolate balls to his staff. The idiot later realized he had been taping himself on my answering machine, and he called me to apologize. I fired him soon after. He was not even that good. He was a legend in his own mind. For some of them, their law degree goes to their heads.

While at the attorney's office, look around the room to see if there are very expensive furnishings, or if there are Persian rugs on the floor. You don't need to pay for it all. If they are very opulent and gaudy, consider not hiring them. This is where your money is going. A main issue to consider is whether they return your phone calls. They should return your call within twenty four hours. If they take three days before they return your calls, get rid of them immediately.

Retainers are very important. You can tell right from the start if you have a bad attorney or not, based on the size of the retainer they are asking for. If they want over $5000 for a retainer, find someone else. Over $5000 for a retainer should be a red flag to you. Twice, I have paid $25,000 for a retainer. In both cases, the attorney lost the case and did a horrible job. These were not complicated cases. In both cases, after hiring a much better attorney, who repaired the damages done by these attorneys, I was charged a much lower retainer.

When discussing the cost of the case, is the attorney reasonable? Are their fees reasonable? What I mean by reasonable is, how much of a retainer are they asking for? In a civil litigation case, as I stated above, if the attorney is asking for any more than $5,000, go find somebody else. If you give more than $5000, you will never see that money again, and you may be stuck with a bad attorney. To determine if you have a decent attorney who is working in your best interest, $5000 gives you enough legal time and hours in which to do that. That is the reason you should not give too large a retainer. You want to know if this is a decent attorney or not. If he/she runs through your retainer without doing much work, than you will know to find another attorney. I cannot stress this enough: pay no more than a $5000 retainer in a civil litigation case. If they start saying it is complicated, or that they are the best, so they need to charge more, go find someone else. Unlike doctors, who are paid by insurance, and at times capped for their services, attorneys are not. You have to cap the attorney.

The gender, nationality, ethnicity, or race of the attorney does not matter. The integrity and ethics of the attorney is what matters. The best attorney I know, attended law school in another country. He came to the United States and passed the bar exam in his respective state.

He did not go to an Ivy League school. He does not wear fancy clothes or shoes, or expensive jewelry. He has won awards, and he deserves them. His abilities by far exceed any of the other attorneys that I've ever worked with. This includes some who were President of the American Academy of Matrimonial Law, as well as President of the International Academy of Matrimonial Law. It also includes the alleged voted state's top best attorneys in their respective fields.

All these labels don't mean anything. I've been with attorneys who have been written up in magazines, and have won awards. What you should know is that these attorneys can pay money to be in these magazines, and they can pay to be given these awards. It does not make them better attorneys. It makes them more expensive attorneys, and if you look again at a lawsuit as an investment, is it really worth spending more money on one attorney as opposed to another, especially since the more expensive attorney may not produce? There are so many attorneys that you can almost look at them as stocks. If one doesn't produce, or go up in value for you, then get rid of him— buy another one that does produce; hence, it goes up in value.

If you are involved in a personal injury case, or a workers' comp case, then the attorney who represents you is most likely working on a contingency basis. They get a percentage of what you receive. In other words, if you don't win, they don't win. In these cases, you will always be the plaintiff in a personal injury case, and the claimant in a workers' comp case. In these cases, you are not being sued, and you don't have to worry about being raped financially by an attorney. These are not necessarily the easiest cases, since the insurance company does not want to pay you for your injuries. They will hire experts to dispute your claims, even if you have serious injuries. There are many good personal injury and workers' comp attorneys, and if they don't win cases and produce good results, they will be out of business. Don't ever give a PI or WC attorney a retainer.

If you are being sued, and you have money and assets, then you need to hire a pitbull. You cannot hire a weak attorney who cannot litigate, and is afraid to offend people. When I was sued by the institution I worked for, I was up against a lot. I was facing an extremely vindictive CEO who was using the institution's money to sue me and others. I was up against very deep pockets. The attorney I hired, who charged me a $25,000 retainer, would not state the fact that the CEO had requested that I do something unethical against my wishes. The attorney, who charged me the $25,000, asked me, "What is the relevance?" He told me that he did not want to include this fact because it may antagonize the other side.

Well, the other side was extremely hostile, and this attorney lost me $10,000 in court. I switched attorneys, and the first thing the new attorney did was to state, in his first motion, that the CEO asked me to do something unethical against my wishes, and that I had refused. The case settled right after he filed this motion. He charged me only a $5000 retainer, not $25,000, and he was extremely effective. He was the pitbull I needed, since I was being sued, and he was not scared of stating the facts and offending somebody. If you are being sued, the odds are the other party does not like you. You will need to hit back at them as hard as you can, in order for them to settle the case.

If you are being sued, and you have no money and assets, then you are entitled to a court appointed attorney. If you have a job, then you probably should get an attorney. Your wages could be garnished if you lose a lawsuit. If someone tries to sue you, and you have nothing, including having no job, then it was probably stupid for them to sue you in the first place. This is the one time you can represent yourself. You should drag the lawsuit out as long as you can. This will cost the other side time and attorney fees. Even if the other side has deep pockets, sadistic people can be cheap, and they don't want to spend money unnecessarily. This can really get them mad or anxious, and you may be able to get money from them to stop the lawsuit. If you do have money and assets, then going to court without an attorney, or representing yourself, could be suicidal.

When working with attorneys, always try to negotiate costs. Try to get an attorney who works on contingency, or partial contingency, which will save you money. It also gives them incentive to win the case, since they will be receiving a percentage of your award.

Do not ever be afraid to switch attorneys or get a second opinion. There are so many of them out there, and they all want your business. It makes no sense to me for an attorney to cheat his client or not treat him well. A law practice is a business, just like any other, and many attorneys appear to be poor businessmen. If you cheat your client, or don't produce well, you will also lose out on possible referrals. I have given my current attorney so much business through referrals that he has made a lot more money from my referrals than from me. My referrals have also given him referrals because of the good work he does. On the other hand, I have never given any of my other twelve attorneys any referrals, and I have told others to stay away from them. In fact, when a friend of mine was going through a divorce, I referred him to my ex-wife's attorney, who had done a much better job than my own at the time.

Another little trick that attorneys try to do is to wait until right before a hearing or trial, and then ask you for a lot of money for them to go to court. This can usually cause great fear and anxiety for a client who ends up paying. When they do this, start looking for another attorney. You may be stuck with them for the hearing, but get rid of them right afterwards.

Unless you already have a friendship or relationship with your attorney, do not go out to dinner with them. In my experience, they are trying to butter you up to get more money out of you. Treat an attorney like an employee or independent contractor. Do not make friends with them or become close to them. They come a dime a dozen. Do not harass them, and do not sleep with them. Act as if they are your employee with specialty training. Tell them what you want and what you expect of them, and pay them to do so—anything else, you are looking for trouble. If you are wondering if they are acting inappropriately, ask yourself, "If I owned a business, and my employee was acting like this, what would I do?" You will have your answer pretty quickly.

The fact is, attorneys are very poorly regulated, and they are allowed to get away with quite a bit. Unlike doctors, they are not scrutinized very much; they have great leeway in taking advantage and ripping off their clients. Not all attorneys do this, but a lot of them do. Many of them do practice unethically, and they appear to be accountable to nobody. I did file a complaint with the Bar Counsel after I originally lost custody of my son. It was funny how the investigator from the Bar Counsel referred to the attorney, who I filed the complaint about, on a first name basis. She did appear hostile to me at times on the phone. They kept the case open for a year, and she told me they took the complaint very seriously, which is why they kept it open for a year and attempted to pursue some of the documents in the case.

Nothing happened to the attorney, and she appeared to have protected him more than anything else. Protecting unethical attorneys just makes things worse for everybody. Poor law is practiced, and the legal profession is looked at in a negative light by the public. Accountability and regulation of attorneys' behavior would only improve the profession, and would bring the best attorneys to the top of everyone's list, while eliminating the poor ones. Going to law school and passing the bar exam does not make a great attorney, or even a good one. Unfortunately, due to the poor regulation and supervision of attorneys, you have to regulate them yourself. Do not give referrals to a bad attorney. You should warn others not to use them. Given that there are so many, you can fire them easily, and find another one. That is the best way of regulating them and holding them accountable.

Review of Chapter

In this chapter, we learned a great deal about choosing attorneys. We learned about red flags of a poor attorney. We also learned that if you do not like an attorney, or have a poor attorney, you should get rid of him/her as quickly as possible. We also learned that you have to be the boss, and treat your attorney as your employee. Even though the attorney is managing the case, you have to be the CEO of your case, and determine if the attorney is doing an adequate job, in which case you will have to make the decision whether to keep the attorney or not.

Now that you have chosen your attorney, you still have to become the CEO of your lawsuit. In order to do that, you have to be strong physically, emotionally, mentally, and spiritually, in order to make tough decisions. In the next chapter, we will see how to maintain your health and your strength during a lawsuit.

Notes

39

Notes

40

Notes

41

Notes

42

CHAPTER 4

Step 4: Keep Yourself Healthy

Lawsuits can be very stressful. They can weigh on somebody physically, emotionally, mentally, and spiritually. In order to win a lawsuit, one has to pay close attention to these four spheres of health. Maintain all of them, and your odds of winning are much greater. The other side is going to try to beat you down emotionally and mentally; through physical and spiritual health, you can maintain mental and emotional strength. I cannot emphasize this enough.

A serious lawsuit, with a lot of money involved, or when the custody of children is involved, can take a great physical toll on people. I have seen people lose weight, or gain weight, and completely let themselves go physically. A client I had, who was in a prolonged divorce, lost a lot of weight. He looked emaciated when he came into my office, only one month after I had previously seen him. Another woman, I knew, lost her voice and could not eat for days after she was served with papers. The lawsuit she was served was excessive, and her reaction to it was physically horrible. She was afraid to leave her house to buy groceries, and began not only losing weight but becoming physically ill. She developed a fever and began vomiting. It was hard to talk to her on the phone because her voice became so raspy, and she would gag while talking. This went on for weeks, until her lawyer settled the case, in which case she regained her normal health. However, during the period of time while the lawsuit ensued, her body appeared to be shutting down, and her defense mechanisms and her immune system appeared to have faltered.

Another person, I know, developed rectal pain during his divorce, and actually went to the hospital emergency room to get his prostate checked. The emergency room staff could not find anything wrong with him, and the ER doctor said that a person with a prostate problem would have hit the roof after receiving the rectal exam he received. This person ended up being admitted to the psychiatric ward because he was diagnosed with severe depression, which was manifesting itself in physical symptoms.

Many times, a severe emotional trauma, such as a lawsuit, can manifest physical symptoms. When I was served with a ten million dollar lawsuit, at first, I was just in disbelief. Then I developed chest pain while I was at work. A coworker asked me if I was OK, and I said that I just felt a little dizzy, and I needed to sit down. The next thing I knew, I was strapped to a stretcher and was being taken to a hospital by ambulance. I ended up being admitted to a coronary care unit and being ruled out for a myocardial infarction (MI), which is a heart attack, in layman's terms. That was an experience.

I was in a room with many patients, all with heart monitors on. I wanted to talk to somebody, so I tried talking to the patient who was in the bed to my left. The only problem was that he was dead. I witnessed gurneys being wheeled in, with medical residents pumping on patients' chests, trying to revive them. It was a nightmare. I wanted to leave, but they would not let me. It turned out that it was a panic attack, and not a heart attack, from being served with a lawsuit. When my son came to bring me home the next day, I began to recover. This particular lawsuit, which caused me this grief, was a drummed up lawsuit by a sadistic human being, who not only did not win the lawsuit, but a couple years later was removed by security from the institution he worked in, never to be allowed back again. The reason I am pointing this out is because a lawsuit, whether real or fabricated, can have great consequences for innocent people. I also want to make it clear that there are sick, deranged people out there, who abuse the legal system as a weapon to hurt others.

As you can see, emotions can become physical, and physical problems can become emotional. Knowing this, a powerful way of getting through a lawsuit, or winning a lawsuit, is to keep yourself in great physical shape. It will allow you to think clearer and greatly challenge the opposing side. Go to the gym and workout. Do so, even more now than before you were in the lawsuit. Hire a personal trainer. In fact, now is the time to be more physical and to get into the best shape of your life. If you like running, then run farther, or more often. Swim farther, or more often. Definitely engage in sports if you can. When I was going through my divorce, I took tennis lessons, and I actually played tennis better than ever at that time. Ironically, when my ex-wife and I were divorcing, we played a tennis match against each other. It was the only time I didn't lose, and I actually won the second set. The third set became a draw, and we were not able to finish due to darkness. This match represented our divorce and custody battle of 13 years, where neither refused to yield.

The reality is, when involved in a lawsuit, and especially when defending yourself, pay attention to your physical health. Watch your diet, and eat nutritiously. Exercise regularly, and do anything to calm yourself. Yoga or the martial arts can be very helpful. Again, go to the gym regularly. The endorphins produced from exercising will help you greatly during your lawsuit. Physical health leads to emotional and mental health, which will benefit you in the courtroom or during depositions. It will benefit you when recalling facts to give to your lawyer, and will help you be clear and articulate if you need to testify. Being physically healthy will help you react, or not react, if things appear to be going against you, and will help you maintain your calm during cross examination.

Besides your physical health, in order to be victorious in a lawsuit, one needs to maintain their mental and emotional health, since the other side, no matter how vindictive or despicable a character they are, will most likely not try to hurt you physically, and cannot really hurt you spiritually. What they will do is try to humiliate and embarrass you, and beat you down emotionally and mentally. That is the opposing counsel's goal. You need to be very aware of this. Do not think that the other side has any values, morally and/or ethically. They don't, when it comes to a lawsuit. Do not think for two seconds that the opposing side and their attorney won't lie and exaggerate. They will. Be prepared for this.

When I was going through my custody battle, I was cross examined by opposing counsel about a concert I had taken my son to when he was eight years old. When I took him to the concert, many of the fans and spectators were telling my son that he was lucky to have a father like me. In fact, we had a great time. However, during cross examination, opposing counsel questioned me on the stand, and asked me if people were using drugs in front of my son. I responded, "No, absolutely not!" He then asked me if one of the band players, during that concert, had screamed into the microphone, "Are you all having a fucking great time?" right in front of my son. I responded, "No, absolutely not." He then said, "I have knowledge that he did say it, right in front of your son." I responded, "I don't see how that is possible, since that band player died a month before we went to the concert, and there was a different band player." Despite the blatant lies, I lost custody of my son at the time, only to regain it a few years later.

This is what opposing counsel will do. They will lie, and they will exaggerate and try to get you to say things that are not true. They will write things about you that are fabricated, and submit those papers to the court to be put on public record. Don't think for two seconds that opposing counsel will ever get punished for blatantly lying and defaming you. They are protected by the legal system. Knowing this will make it easier for you to get through the lawsuit. Remember that lying and deception is part of the process, and opposing counsel is just doing his or her job and trying to win at any cost. If this gets to you, and you are thin-skinned, then you will have a tough time winning a lawsuit, let alone surviving a lawsuit. You must maintain emotional and mental fortitude throughout. I learned this the hard way. There was a time, while I was in court, that I could not stand listening to the lies being said about me on the stand. I told my lawyer I was leaving, and he responded by punching me under the table. He said that I was to sit there and listen, and do nothing. This is how you need to act to win. You need to maintain your emotional and mental health, and be *Teflon*.

In order to maintain your mental and emotional health, treat yourself well. Get massages, manicures, and pedicures. Take saunas and steam baths. Go to the gym, and sit in the hot tub and Jacuzzi. If you can, vacation and enjoy life. Besides maintaining emotional and mental fortitude, it will piss off the opposing side and rattle them. When the institution was suing me, I went to Florida to watch a professional baseball team play during spring training. Although I was distraught at the time, this certainly helped, and it showed that I would never give in to the institution.

It is important for your emotional well being to maintain a strong support system. True friends and supportive family members are very important. When I was going through my custody battle, my aunt was so supportive of me; she was proofreading and helping me write my motions. By the way, she was 100 years old at the time, and living independently. Talk about great support. Many friends were there for me, and I usually had someone to talk to. The one issue that can come up is that you can become obsessed with your legal situation, and that may be all you talk about. It can turn people off. Therefore, you must compartmentalize your situation, and enjoy other aspects of life. Do not let your legal situation consume you. You need to relax. Maintain an active sex life. If necessary, masturbate more, just to relieve tension. It will help in these times of great stress. There was one time I had to appear in court against my ex-wife, and a good female friend of mine gave me oral sex in my living room, right before I drove to the courthouse. Neither the opposing counsel nor the judge could bother me that day. I did very well in court that day. If possible, I recommend it.

If necessary, go to a therapist. This can be very helpful. It is always good to be able to vent and get things out. However, you have to be careful with this. One would think that going to a therapist, during a time of great stress, would be a wise thing to do. It is the appropriate and wise thing to do. However, it could be used against you. If the other side gets wind that you are seeing a therapist, they will try to use this to say that you are unstable, especially if you are in a custody battle. You definitely should stay away from psychiatric medications, like antidepressants, because that will certainly be used against you. When I was going through my divorce, I was questioned about a time I went to see a counselor when I was in college. I only went twice, and it occurred a decade before I was married. Yet this was brought up, and I was questioned about it in court. One thing I can say is, do not take personally anything that is said against you by the other side. Certainly, do not start believing them, which is what they want. If a lie is told enough times, it starts appearing true to whoever is listening. Do not fall into this. Politicians are experts at this.

There is a way around this therapist issue. Start seeing a life coach. They are not licensed mental health workers, and there is no mental health record. Some coaches do much better jobs than many therapists. If you are asked, in court, if you are receiving mental health treatment, you can honestly say no. Also, instead of a therapist, what I have found more helpful is taking personal development and professional development courses, in addition to having a life coach. Therapists tend to dwell on the past, and continuously bring up past traumas, which just makes you feel worse. A coach will focus on the future and setting goals for yourself. Nobody knows what will happen in the future, but being clear in mind and thought will help you shape and create it. Bringing the past up, over and over again, will only make you fearful and sad. That is why I prefer coaching over therapy, and the opposing side cannot do much with it to claim that you are unstable.

Another important means of maintaining your emotional and mental health is to maintain your spiritual health. I firmly believe that physical, emotional, mental, and spiritual realms are all interconnected. If you improve one realm, all three others will improve. When I say spiritual, I don't necessarily mean religious. Spirituality raises questions; religion gives answers, which are really opinions, with no basis for real truth. God is not on anyone's side, although people like to claim this. God is here for everyone. There is no evidence to support God favoring one over another, except when claimed by the mentally ill or sociopaths. God is not a Republican or a Democrat. There is nothing wrong with praying. It is very helpful and, once again, can lead to questions being asked when answers are not always present.

Experiencing the beauty of nature is very helpful during a stressful situation. Before the current administration destroys all of it by dumping soot from coal mining operations, try to get out and enjoy the forests, rivers, and streams, and the sky with the heavens above us. This is all very spiritual, and will make your problems appear to be less than they are. I used to walk on the beach and look out at the ocean when I was going through a lawsuit. Looking at the beauty of the water, and the vastness of the oceans, will make your legal issues appear much smaller, and with less meaning.

One thing you must never do, especially when going through a lawsuit, is to use drugs or alcohol. This can only hurt you. It will affect you emotionally and mentally. From a legal strategic standpoint, you are cutting your throat by doing this. If the other side finds out, it will certainly be used against you, and will certainly hurt you in court. One lawyer once told me that a wise way of approaching a lawsuit is to assume that the other side is watching you at all times, and listening in on your telephone conversations. Live a clean, wholesome life. You can even assume that the other side is videotaping you.

I do not condone faking injuries to make money in a lawsuit, but if you are claiming severe back pain from a car accident, and then go to the gym or help your neighbor move heavy furniture, you are essentially showing the other side how fraudulent you are. If you do this in front of other people, you are creating witnesses against you. If you are truly ill and injured, then you better appear that way, and listen to every instruction your attorney is telling you. If you have to go for physical therapy, then do so.

Finally, since it is good to assume that you are being watched and monitored, it is good advice not to talk or communicate with the other side. They want to win and show that you have no credibility, or destroy the credibility that you do have. The other side either does not want to give up money or property, or is trying to get money or property. That is the way you should view them, especially in a divorce and custody case. These can be very acrimonious, and there are others besides your ex-spouse involved. Unless absolutely necessary, DO NOT SPEAK with your ex-spouse and try to negotiate. Everything must be done through attorneys. Speaking with, and negotiating with, your ex-spouse or opposing party in an adversarial lawsuit, can cost you severely. They are not sincere in their speaking, and everything you tell them will go back to their attorney, who will then strategize against you.

Review of Chapter

In this chapter, we learned how important it is to maintain your physical, emotional, psychological, and spiritual health during a lawsuit. A lawsuit can be a very stressful time in one's life, and one must not neglect their own health during this time.

We learned numerous strategies for maintaining our health during a stressful period, and that maintaining our health can lead to better results in the lawsuit itself.

In the next chapter, we will learn, once embroiled in a lawsuit, that it is always better to negotiate with an out-of-court settlement rather than going to court, and potentially a trial, which is extremely costly and time- consuming.

Notes

52

Notes

53

Notes

54

CHAPTER 5

Step 5: Negotiate

The best way to win a lawsuit is to settle out of court. Once a case is filed, it can be a very time-consuming, expensive, and frustrating process. Once you go to court, all bets are off, and it becomes a crapshoot. You lose a lot of control, and the outcome depends on a third party, the judge, or jury. Some attorneys are expert negotiators, and others are just awful. It is always better to negotiate from a position of power. Unfortunately, the side with more money and time usually has more power. That is the way our legal system works. It favors the wealthy over the poor or middle class; therefore, it does not necessarily bring about justice. The reason for this is simply that if you have more money, you can buy more legal hours, and run the other side out of money.

I had an attorney who once said to me, as he held his left hand above his head, "When you negotiate, you want to be up here," and he further said, as he held his right hand at his waist, "And you want them to be down there." He further said, "Right now, it's the opposite." Basically, I wasn't in any position to negotiate, so I had to choose litigation.

Circumstances can change during the process, where one side would not negotiate at the beginning, and would just want to litigate; but later, they may be more than happy to negotiate and end things. I believe, with negotiation, there are three major issues involved: time, money, and reputation.

People write books on negotiation, and use different techniques. I am no expert on it, and you probably are not either. That is why you hire an attorney. They are supposed to negotiate for you. As I think back to the many cases I was involved in, I can describe the negotiations, and what worked and what did not work.

First off, do not negotiate on your own. Once you hire an attorney, all negotiations need to go through your attorney. One thing this does is remove a lot of the emotion involved. This way, you are not speaking directly to the parties involved on the other side of the lawsuit. As I mentioned in a previous chapter, especially in the case of divorce and custody, if attorneys are involved, do not speak with your ex-spouse. Let the attorneys speak to each other for you. If you are being sued, or are suing somebody, there is surely tension between you and the other party— and why would you want to speak with them anyway?

During negotiations, you do need to express to your attorney exactly what you want, and exactly what you are willing to settle for. You should write this down and have it in front of you when speaking with your attorney. In fact, every time you call your attorney and speak with them, prep yourself for the call. You will be charged for the call. Write down the questions you want to ask the attorney, and ask them. This way, you won't miss out on anything. You don't want to forget something and have to call your attorney back, and then get billed again for it.

The best thing for you to do, during negotiations, is keep your mouth shut, and let your lawyer negotiate for you. Anything you say or do can be used against you, so the less you say during the process, and especially during negotiations, is important. When I say keep your mouth shut, I mean with the other side. Don't get me wrong; open your mouth plenty to your attorney. Make sure your attorney does not miss anything. Your case is not their only case, and you probably know your case, and what you want, better than your attorney does.

In the end, it is up to you to decide if you are willing to settle for what is being offered in the negotiations. You will end up with what you tolerate. If you want more, than tolerate less.

Although I am not an expert at negotiations, I have witnessed so many tactics and techniques from both sides during negotiations, and I can describe many of them to you. The best type of negotiations are win-win situations, where both parties are satisfied with the outcome. This does not always happen and, in some people's minds, the only negotiations they are happy with is *winner take all*. That is called greed, and usually bites you in the ass in the end. Of course, on the other side of greed is fear, and when too fearful, you can give in too easily, and give up everything—and that bites you in the ass immediately.

In the end, a lot depends on your values, your emotional stability, and what you are willing to accept. For example, during my divorce, at first I wanted sole custody of my three-year-old son. As the legal process went on, and I saw how prejudiced the judge was against fathers, I realized that this was not going to happen. I say that the judge was prejudiced because, during a hearing, she said to me, and everyone else in the courtroom, "Don't tell me how to parent a child. I am a divorced mother of two." First off, this statement is ludicrous. It has no place in court, and shows how she should not be hearing custody cases. She may be the divorced mother of two, but who says she is any good at it? She is allowing her personal situation of being a divorced mother have an impact on the case. The reason I bring this up is because I had to alter what I was willing to settle for because I saw how biased the judge was. I ended up settling for a liberal visitation schedule, instead of physical custody, because of the judge's prejudice at the time.

This is a problem with going to court. You do not know who you are going to get as a judge; and, in my particular case, this particular judge was trying to force a settlement for her own personal reasons.

This was the first time I had ever been to court, and it dawned on me that this was an arena that was not objective, and it appears that everyone has their own motives—it was certainly not what I thought. Unfortunately, instead of being impartial in this case, the judge was forcing negotiations. As I found out later, she likes to have dispositions to make herself look better. You have to decide if you want a judge to make a major decision in your life. This is why negotiations are very important.

Two other events happened in this case, which should be noted. As the case continued, and it appeared that I would not gain physical custody of my son, I had to fight to prevent the relocation of my son to a few states away from me. My lawyer at the time said this would not happen, although he, of course, was more interested in how much money he could get out of me before I ran out, since my ex-wife's family had much more than I did at the time. It became apparent that this judge wanted a settlement for her own selfish reasons, and used the relocation to try to force me to settle. At one point as the trial went on, the judge called me and my attorney to the bench. She instructed the court stenographer to stop typing, and said to me and my attorney, "If you try this case, I am going to let your ex-wife relocate to another state."

Now, I had my back against the wall, since my ex-wife would not settle without relocation. My instincts then kicked in. Somewhere inside of me, my mind was telling me that this nasty, unethical judge was threatening me, so I should respond accordingly. I looked her in the face, and said to her, "Let's try the case." My lawyer then said to me, "I see what we are up against." So the trial was set for a later date. I spoke to my lawyer the next day, and said, "Isn't there something you can do about this judge, after what she said." He responded, "Said what?" All of a sudden, my lawyer came down with a case of selective amnesia. It became clear that he did not care how much money he was paid; he cared about his reputation, and the fact that he may appear before this judge again, so he did not want to request the judge recuse herself after doing something so unethical. He was okay with going ahead with the case, since he would get paid; however, to do the right thing for his client was another story.

In this same case, the judge met with both parties, their attorneys, and guardian ad litem, in a diner. Again, she was trying to force a settlement. I have never really heard of this before, or after, for that matter. There was no stenographer, and nothing was on the record. I asked my lawyer, "Is this typical?" He answered, "It happens," while he was charging me the whole time by the hour so he could fill his face with food, and accomplish nothing. Nothing really came out of that, except both lawyers and the guardian ad litem made a killing, financially. This judge was simply trying to force an outcome when she clearly saw that I was not willing to give in to my ex-wife's demands to relocate with my son.

During the trial, as the case continued, it was very apparent that the judge was extremely biased. She would scratch certain statements off the record and, at one point, my lawyer said to me, "This is ridiculous. I see what is going on here." I told him that I wanted to settle the case. I didn't really get what I wanted, but my son was not able to relocate for a year. I was pretty badly beaten and had to give in a lot, including the relocation of my son, which should have never happened, except for the selfishness and unethical behavior of the judge.

Eventually, many years later, I would regain custody of my son, and he relocated to live with me. Ironically, two decades later, I am good friends with a family court judge, in the same county I was divorced in. Unlike the judge in my case, she is a very responsible, fair, and intelligent person. She would not allow the relocation of a child based on her own desires to get a disposition. It is amazing how life can change. There was a period of time when I was very resentful towards judges—now I am very close friends with one. Our legal system deserves fair, honest judges, who really care about people and justice, not ones who have their own agenda.

I have another example of why it is important to negotiate, and why court can be a large risk. Fortunately, I save my emails, but what I am about to illustrate shows the potential corruptness of the legal system. The following is an actual email from my attorney, sent to my ex-wife's attorney (with the names changed).

Nellie,
Here is the first cut of a stipulation. I did not include the provisions we discussed concerning Mr. Snow's serving as a parent-chaperone on class trips, and his meeting with his son and the guidance counselor, because it's not clear to me that we can commit the school to anything in this. However, if you have some language you would like to suggest, perhaps expressing our intent, I'll be happy to have your input.
Talk to you soon.
Regards,

Nellie is my ex-wife's attorney. The names are fake to protect the guilty. My attorney is writing to her about drafting up a stipulation. You can imagine that Nellie had nothing nice to say in court about my parenting skills and, at times, was arguing to the court that I should have supervised visitation. Supervised visitation is given to parents who are felt to be unsafe around their children.

However, when you look at these next two emails, a mother, named Nellie, is asking me to pick up her two children—one of the children was my son's age, and the other was younger than my son.

Mr. Snow,
Our babysitter had a death in her family, and can't get JR to the game today. I understand that you are taking your son from Jamie's house. Would it be possible for you to give JR and Jacob a ride to the game

*from Jamie's house? Harry will be meeting them there, and I am going
to try my best to get there, but it won't be until later.*
Thank you.

The second email from the same parent is:

Thanks. I know JR will want to participate.
Nellie

This email had to do with my showing baseball training videos to
the little league team that Nellie's son was on.

The ironic issue here is that the attorney, Nellie, in the first email,
is the parent, Nellie, in the second two emails. You see, I was a little
league coach, and I happened to be the coach of my son, along with
Nellie's sons. As you can see, the same attorney/parent who is
requesting the court give me supervised visitation with my own son,
because she argued that I am not safe to be alone with my son, is at
the same time asking me to not only coach her children but to pick
them up and drive them to the game.

Now, I complained vehemently to my own attorneys, who did
nothing about this situation. They apparently were friendly with my
ex-wife's attorney, or perhaps had some internal, unethical code that
they all adhered to. My ex-wife's attorney should have been thrown
off the case, and her emails should have been used as evidence against
my ex-wife, but none of this occurred. Anyway, this demonstrates the
many risks of using the legal system, and why it is far better to settle
out of court if you can.

The bottom line is that court and the legal system are very
unpredictable. As you can see, there are other factors besides the facts
of the case. There are people involved, many of which have their own
agenda. There are politics involved, and lawyers do have lunch with
judges. I have witnessed this. Going to court, even if it appears to be

a surefire case, can end up a losing case. It is always better to settle out of court. There are less people involved, and less agendas involved.

62

Review of Chapter

In this chapter, we learned that it is always best to settle out of court if possible. You will most likely get the best results, closest to what you are seeking. There are many factors, people, and agendas if you do not settle, and pursue litigation.

If you are unfamiliar with the legal system, and feel that the courts will bring you justice, then guess again. The court system is filled with bias, politics, and people with their own inherent agendas. Their agendas may not coincide with what you want, or even with the facts of the case. Always settle outside if possible, and always hire a lawyer who knows how to negotiate.

If you are unable to settle, and/or the other side is absolutely unreasonable, which can happen, then you have no choice but to go to court and litigate. Your lawyer should know how to deal with the court system procedurally. In the next chapter, we will discuss how you, as a client, should behave in the courtroom.

Notes

Notes

Notes

66

CHAPTER 6

Step 6: Litigation and Going to Court

Appearing in court can be very intimidating and scary for somebody who has never done so before. As I had said in the previous chapter, an out-of-court settlement is always best, and one should try to avoid appearing in court if possible. I have been to court many times, and I have been given a lot of advice by attorneys on how to behave in court. Your attorney does most of the talking, so it is best to say nothing unless requested to. My experience is that attorneys will usually give you good advice on how to behave in court, since they have their own reputation to uphold.

One attorney once told me that you are in court from the minute you wake up in the morning. In other words, assume you are being observed in your own home, from the second you wake up. This will prepare you well for court.

After you wake up, conduct yourself in a professional manner. In other words, bathe or shower, fix your hair, shave if you are male, and make yourself up to look very professional. Appearance and presentation is extremely important and should not be ignored. Dress conservatively and neatly. A dark suit for men with a white shirt and red tie is always good. Women should dress in a conservative dress, and essentially wear business attire. Make sure your clothes are neatly pressed. Do not wear flashy jewelry or fancy watches. The people in the courtroom are not paid that well, except the attorneys, so wearing a Rolex in court is not going to benefit you.

I have seen people dress like complete slobs in the courtroom. It never benefits them, and the way the court treats them is very different than the way the court treats someone who is professionally dressed. Although judges and court personnel do their best to remain neutral, it is human nature to judge others. We all do that, and somebody neatly dressed and coiffed will be treated differently than someone with an undershirt and ripped jeans. I even know a judge who told me that a person's appearance can affect her decision.

Eat a healthy breakfast, and do not spill any food or beverage on yourself. If you do, you will be self-conscious in court. Make sure your fly or zipper is zipped up. If you are a man, make sure your tie is straight and neat. If you are a woman, I would not show much cleavage, or wear a provocative dress. This will not work for you in this venue, with either a male or female judge. Conservative is the best for court.

Whenever I drove to court, I took my Honda, and not my BMW. You do not want to come off as flashy. I always obeyed the speed limits when I drove, and I would always arrive early. If your lawyer tells you to meet them early, then come even earlier than they told you to. You will feel better knowing you are at the courthouse earlier than just on time. You definitely do not want to be late. Refrain from using obscenities, from the time you wake up until the time you leave the courthouse later in the day. This is good practice. Do not use any drugs or drink any alcohol. I would even refrain from using anti-anxiety medication, such as Xanax or klonopin. If you are nervous before you go to court, then meditate, exercise, do yoga, or have sex. These actually really help. If you don't have a partner, masturbate. It will relax you and take your mind off of court—although it is hard to get stimulated sexually if you are thinking of court. In fact, it's probably good birth control to think about court.

When you get to the courthouse, be polite and professional to everyone. Say *please, thank you,* and *excuse me.* Do not cause a scene.

This is not a place to start arguments or fights. You will most likely pass through a metal detector, similar to the ones at airports. Do not be taken aback by this. It is for everyone's safety, including your own. There are many crazy people out there who can show up at a courthouse with a weapon, for either vengeful or political reasons, so be grateful for the security guards there. They are usually very nice people.

After I arrive at the courthouse, EARLY, I usually look for a posting on the wall that tells you which courtroom you are in, and what time it starts. The courtroom is usually accurate, but the time is usually way off. If you are very lucky, you can be called quickly as one of the first few cases, and be out of the courtroom early. If you are unlucky, you can be there all day, listening to other cases before you. This can be either fascinating or torture, depending on how you view it. Here is where court can be very stressful if you are new to it.

You need to understand, although other cases in court may be interesting to listen to, you are paying your hard earned money to listen to those cases, which have nothing to do with your case. Your lawyer is charging you by the hour for the courtroom appearance, whether he/she is doing anything or not. He/she is also charging you for travel time to get from his/her home or office to the courthouse. Any expert witnesses also need to be paid for their time, and the odds are, unless you are on contingency, you are also paying for them by the hour. The best way to deal with this is to hope for the best and prepare for the worst, as one lawyer once told me. Be prepared to pay for a full day in court, even if it does not happen. Sitting in the courthouse and hoping your case gets called early, because it is more expensive if it gets called late, can drive you crazy. The best advice is *fuhgettaboutit!!!* Prepare yourself to pay for the whole day, and for your case to be called last.

When you are in the courthouse, you should wait for your attorney, and meet him/her outside the courtroom. Your lawyer should tell you where to meet him/her. Some may want to meet outside the courthouse. Do not speak with the opposing party or counsel. The odds are, since you are in court, it is contentious and heated, and you do not want to start a scene. There are times when you may be proceeding through the metal detector, and the opposing side or opposing counsel may be right in front of you or behind you in line. Do not start up or say anything. Be polite and smile as needed. At some point, you will see the opposing side and counsel. Once again, be professional. There was one time I saw my ex-father-in-law in the courthouse, and I was about to run over to curse him out but, luckily, we all got called into the courtroom before that could happen. Thank God, that happened; because, had I cursed him out, it would have been brought to the judge's attention, and it would not have fared well for me. It may be very hard, but CONTROL YOUR EMOTIONS, no matter if you are being treated unfairly or not.

You must act professionally, and say as little as possible when around opposing parties or counsel. There was one time when my attorney, my ex-wife's attorney, my ex-wife, and I were standing outside of the courthouse speaking. My ex-wife's attorney said to my attorney, "You can't do that." I responded by saying, "Whenever you say you can't do that, and point at someone, it means you have one finger pointing at who you are saying that to, and three fingers pointing towards yourself, meaning, "I can't do that." I pointed with my index finger, and curled my other fingers backward to display the point. My ex-wife's attorney then wrote up in court papers that I made my hand look like a gun, and pointed it at him and my ex-wife, threatening them. You see, attorneys are so full of crap that you really should never say anything to the opposing attorney, no matter what. The only exception is cross-examination, when you have to respond to them, and I will give some great guidelines for that.

When inside the courthouse, just try to keep a straight poker face. This is especially important in the courtroom. Sit with your attorney and be quiet. Do not joke around, speak up, or be overly fidgety. If you are anxious, tell your attorney, and perhaps he/she can calm you down, or you can leave the courtroom, but be aware of when your case is called. You want to be present when the judge or his/her assistant calls your case. If you are in the courtroom before the judge arrives, then stand up when the bailiff announces the judge's entry. Just be courteous, kind, and professional. The judge is an authority figure. If you have issues with authority figures, then now is the time to deal with it and suck it up. The judge can make decisions that can affect your life for years to come. Remember, you chose to litigate and pass the decision-making process on to this authority figure. I am not an expert on judge's personalities, but they vary to a great degree. One thing I can tell you is, don't judge a book by its cover. It doesn't matter if your judge is black or white, red or yellow, male or female, tall or short, or old or young. What matters is the decisions they have made in the past, which really speaks to what their opinions and stands on issues are. Another important factor, which is not usually mentioned, is the judge's relationship with your attorney. In one case I was going through, I had a very well known and respected attorney. However, it became apparent that the judge did not like him, which did not fare well for me at the time. Believe it or not, the judges and attorneys know each other, and how each feels about the other is an important factor. Once again, the facts of the case are not the only variable to the judge's decision. Again, think negotiation if possible, even after litigation has started.

One attorney told me that judges are human, and they make human decisions. This is obviously true. He said, "A judge could have an upset stomach from something he/she ate, and/or be in a bad mood that day, and make decisions based on that, so you never know what could happen. Without going into detail, I was in court one day, and it was after a certain major league baseball team won the World Series. The judge was wearing a cap of that team. It was already known in that courtroom that I was from a different city, where another major league baseball team was from, which was a rival of the team that won the World Series. My first reaction, when I saw the judge wearing the cap, was, "Oh, shit!!!" Needless to say, I do not like the team the judge was wearing the cap for. I don't know if that had any influence on the judge's decisions that day, but it certainly affected my psychological state, especially since I really did not like that particular judge prior to this incident.

You may have to go to court many times once litigation begins: for pre-trial hearings; motions to be heard and answered; meetings with the judge, for no apparent reason, except to make you spend more money; and if it comes down to it, for a trial. A trial can last many days and, at times, it can be split up. So, it can start for two days in May, and end with another three days in June, for example. The trial itself is very costly, but the preparation for the trial may be even more costly. This is why negotiation is so important.

There are times when a case may require juries to make decisions, instead of judges. That depends on the case and the attorneys. I have never been involved in a case that requires a jury, but those cases will be much longer, and even more expensive since jury selection is required. The interesting thing about these cases is that the case can be won almost based on the jury selection, and there are experts out there who know how to choose jurors properly. This is beyond the scope of my knowledge, so I will just mention it here. Just know this could happen in civil cases, and you should discuss the advantages and disadvantages with your attorney.

The times you will have to speak in court are when you are being examined by your lawyer, or cross-examined by opposing counsel. This also applies when being deposed outside of the courtroom. Let's leave court for a minute and talk about depositions. Once litigation has started, when dealing with the opposing side or counsel, act with them as if you are in the courtroom. Always be professional, and always watch what you say. It took me a while to understand this, but what goes on the record is what the judge uses to make a decision. When I say *on the record*, I mean what is said in court, and recorded by the stenographer, as well as what paper evidence is presented to the court, and accepted.

Once a lawsuit begins, there is a period of time called *Discovery*. This is when both parties attempt to get evidence to support their respective cases. Lawyers get their evidence and facts to present to the judge in a number of ways. One way is what you tell them or write up for them. Another is any documents that you give them. Lawyers also need to obtain information from the opposing side in order to present the facts to the court. They can do this in a number of ways. One is by observing the opposing party and reporting what they see to the court. Another is by subpoenaing papers from the other party in which they have to present. These documents are paper documents, and could be emails as well, so always be careful what you put in an email. Emails are discoverable.

If someone withholds papers and evidence from the opposing party or court, they could be liable for civil contempt of court. Contempt of court refers to actions that either defy a court's authority, cast disrespect on the court, or impede the ability of the court to perform its function.

Contempt takes two forms: criminal contempt and civil contempt. Actions that one might associate with the phrase, *contempt of court,* such as a party causing a serious disruption in the courtroom, yelling at the judge, or refusing to testify before a grand jury, would often constitute criminal contempt of court.

Civil contempt of court most often happens when someone fails to adhere to an order from the court, with resulting injury to a private party's rights. For example, failure to pay court-ordered child support can lead to punishment for civil contempt. Civil contempt of court may be *direct* or *indirect*. Direct contempt occurs in the presence of the court—during a court proceeding, for example. Indirect contempt occurs outside the presence of the court.

Civil contempt often occurs indirectly—for example, when a party is ordered to turn over financial records within thirty days but refuses to do so. Those held in civil contempt generally must be given notice of the sanctions, and an opportunity to be heard. The bottom line is that you want to avoid this, and be honest with the courts and not withhold evidence.

Another way attorneys obtain information from the opposing parties is through interrogatories. These are questionnaires that opposing counsel will send to your attorney that you have to fill out. You are filling these forms out under oath and, therefore, need to be truthful. Do not lie or leave things out on these. However, do not volunteer any additional information unless asked to.

The other way attorneys obtain evidence is through depositions. This is where you are asked questions by opposing counsel, and you answer these questions under oath. Your attorney is present during these depositions, and can object to the questioning. Your attorney may be deposing the other party on the same day you are being deposed, or it can be spread out over time. These depositions usually take place at one of the attorney's offices. When being deposed, you are under oath, so tell the truth. In an ideal world, this would happen, but I have witnessed so many people lying under oath, and nothing ever happens to them. I don't recommend lying because you can always be caught lying, and it can hurt your case, but I never saw anyone get in trouble for perjury, although I assume it happens. In any case, do not lie. Tell the truth under oath, whether in court or being deposed. Prior to being deposed, you will be sworn in; or, if not religious, you can affirm instead of swearing. I have seen lawyers make an issue about this, but there is supposed to be a separation between church and state, so I don't know what their problem is.

Anyway, the best way to handle cross-examination is not to say anything in addition to answering the question. I have been coached many times on cross- examination, and I learned how to do this. There are always one of four answers that you can give: yes, no, I don't know, or I don't remember. Do not answer anything else unless specifically asked. If you do answer additional information, it can cost you your case. Do not get emotional, and do not blurt out your answer right away. When the opposing attorney asks you a question, repeat it to yourself at least once, and preferably twice, before answering: yes, no, I don't know, or I don't remember. Take your time and do not rush. You probably dislike or hate your opposing counsel, but despite this, do not get emotional. It is the opposing counsel's job to try to get you emotional and shock you into saying something you do not want to say. Once the deposition is over, it will be transcribed, and you will have the opportunity to review it and make any corrections on it. The deposition is not part of the court record, but it can be used during cross- examination in court, since your deposition statements were made under oath.

Returning to court, evidence is presented to court, with either paperwork or testimony. Paperwork needs to be submitted to the court, usually as exhibits, and needs to be accepted or admitted as evidence. Testimony is through direct examination and cross-examination of the parties, as well as direct and cross- examination of witnesses and expert witnesses. Your attorney should know how to perform direct and cross-examinations. Your attorney will prep you prior to going to court on this process. Your attorney will want certain things on the record—meaning recorded by the court stenographer— for the judge to review, and other things not on the record, which the opposing counsel probably will want on record.

Direct examination and cross-examination in the courtroom is unique in many ways from being deposed. The two are similar in that both are done under oath, and you are sworn in or affirmed for both. It is considered perjury if you lie either way but most likely worse in court. Whatever is said in court, as long as the stenographer is recording, is considered *on the record.* Depositions are not on the record but can be referred to by attorneys during examination and cross- examination in the courtroom. What is put on the record is very important. The judge will use this information to make his/her decision, and will refer to what is *on the record* to back up the decision. If you don't agree with or like the judge's decision, then what is *on the record* can be used to appeal the judge's decision, in which case arguments are then presented to a higher court, usually the appellate court, and so on. Appeals and so forth are beyond the scope of this book, but be aware that they are very costly if you decide to pursue it.

When testifying in the courtroom, as always, be very professional and polite. Dress appropriately and professionally. Sit up straight and don't slump over or lean forward too much. I was told not to do that by one of my attorneys. Don't speak unless spoken to, or asked to answer questions. If the judge asks a question, answer it. When speaking to a judge, always respond to them as *Your Honor*, *Sir* or *Ma'am*. *Your Honor* is always preferable, and it shows great respect for the court. There are many more people present in the courtroom than during a deposition. Most importantly, the judge is there, and in some cases, the jury. There may be family members or strangers present. Witnesses are usually not allowed in the courtroom until called, so as not to bias their testimony. There also may be others watching the case, including the media.

Your attorney will ask you questions first, and you should answer them appropriately, the way you and he/she prepared you to answer them. Every attorney prepares their clients for testimony, and you should have practiced this already before ever getting to this point. The other side can object or request items be struck(removed) from the record. The judge will decide if an objection is appropriate (sustained), or not appropriate (overruled). The best advice for direct examination is to practice with your attorney, since you know what questions will be asked. It is important to practice because your attorney may know a better way of answering the question than you do. It is possible that you do know the answer but, as human nature is, you could be leaving something important out, and your attorney will want what may have been left out, to be on the record. Many times, things will come back to you on the stand that you have already practiced. If you don't practice, you could miss items or statements that are vital to your case. There may also be items or statements your attorney does not want on the record, and having not practiced prior opens you up for putting unwanted statements on the record.

Cross-examination is the most challenging. You need to be prepared for everything, and expect anything. They can bring up something that happened to you twenty years before, and you are expected to answer. During my divorce, the opposing counsel asked me, "Weren't you on antidepressants and seeking psychiatric help during college?" I responded, "What?" At first, I was a little shocked. Then, I responded, "No, I saw the student services counselor one or two times about some anxiety over my upcoming finals." This is an example of how attorneys can distort things and exaggerate things, and how they can bring up things twenty years prior to try to discredit you. Again, just stick to *yes, no, I don't know, and I don't remember,* no matter what they throw at you. Always: YES, NO, I DON'T KNOW, and I DON'T REMEMBER. Your attorney can object or comment to help you during cross-examination.

Another time, while I was being cross examined, the opposing counsel, who was weird and aggressive to begin with, got too close to me on the witness stand, and my attorney had to speak up and tell the court that the opposing counsel was in my space and should not get that physically close to me. Another time, I was cross examined by two attorneys at once, although I found out later that should have never happened, and was inappropriate. My point is, anything can happen, so don't be shocked by it. Once you are through with cross-examination, your attorney can do a redirect examination, addressing some of the points brought out in cross-examination.

When you are finished testifying, go back and sit down with your attorney. Be quiet, professional, and polite. Do not lunge at or start an argument with opposing counsel, even if you want to. There are other very stressful times in the courtroom that you need to be aware of. This includes when opposing parties are testifying and being directly examined and cross examined. People lie and make up things, even under oath. Some even believe their own lies, since they have been lying to themselves for years. Do not get upset by what you hear. Just take notes and jot down things you want to tell your attorney, especially if witnesses are lying. You actually know your case the best, even better than your attorney, and you can help your attorney by feeding him/her questions to ask the opposing party, or hostile witnesses and expert witnesses, under cross-examination.

Hostile expert witnesses do exist. They are described as either *hired guns* (purposefully hostile and/or lying), since they are getting paid by one party, or just incompetent and stupid (not hired by either party, and probably court appointed), and not getting paid by either party, or possibly getting paid by both parties. Both are equally as harmful. Now, don't get me wrong; there are very good expert witnesses who tell the truth and know how to do their job. On the other hand, I have seen others in their own little narcissistic worlds, who just make up things, whether they are real or not. I once saw an alleged expert neurologist make up his own diagnosis of a patient, although the diagnosis was not generally accepted by anyone in the medical community, except himself.

There was one time I was sitting in court, and the witness on the stand was not only blatantly lying about me but lying about the relationship he had with both me and the other party. I said to my attorney, "I can't listen to this shit anymore; I'm leaving." My attorney actually punched me in the leg, under the table, and said to me, "You will do no such thing. You will sit here and take notes, and shut your mouth." He was absolutely right, and I was letting my emotions get to me. First off, had I left the room, I would have had to stand up and walk out of the courtroom, right in front of the judge during testimony, which would have made me look pretty bad. Secondly, I was able to pull myself together and take notes on the perjured statements, and hand my notes to my attorney, which he used on cross-examination to discredit this hostile witness. Had I left the room, I would not have been able to help my attorney. Lawsuits are emotional and can get very nasty. You need to control your emotions in order to present yourself well to the court, and in order to help your attorney and your case. You want the other side to say ridiculous things, and lie, so they can tie their own noose and hang themselves. Don't get upset by what they say. You should be happy if they say it, if it is not true.

After the testimony is over and the exhibits are in, and the closing statements have been made, the judge or jury makes a decision. In the case of a judge, this can take anywhere from the same day to a couple of weeks later. Juries go out and deliberate, and then come back with a verdict. The time can vary with this too. I have never been in front of a jury—only judges.

Since I wrote a whole chapter on lawyers, I would like to write a little bit about judges. Like any other profession, there are good judges and bad judges. When I say this, I can not base it on their decisions. As far as their decisions are concerned, some I liked, and some I did not like. However, their arguments for their decisions can be revealing. Their decisions are usually backed up by what is on the record, so you can see if they are taking everything into account or are biased towards one side or another. You simply have to review their decision and review the record to see what they included in their decision, and what they did not.

I have had the privilege of being in court with many judges, being on the positive or negative side of their decision. I have had personal friendships with judges, who I have had lunch with and picked their brains. Judges are human beings, and you have to realize that. Some are behind the bench because they want to serve the community and really take their work seriously. Their job is not easy; almost every day, they have to make decisions that really affect people's lives. They can make people pay money, lose custody of their children, or even put somebody behind bars if necessary. With that type of authority, one would think a judge should be a fair and impartial person. For the most part, that is the case.

Judges make less money than many lawyers, so they are usually not going into the field for money. Lawyers, on the other hand, usually are. Some judges really do believe in justice and fairness, and that is why they are behind the bench. Unfortunately, others are on power trips; they abuse their power and can hurt innocent people. Unfortunately, I have witnessed judges who are biased and take out their own issues on the parties in front of them. I have asked other judges about the behaviors of a judge I faced, and I have been told by them that this judge's behavior was extremely inappropriate.

A good judge would listen to both sides, look over the evidence, and then make a decision one way or the other. They would not use any bias or prejudice, and they would keep their own issues out of it. In my divorce case, I had a judge whose behaviors were very questionable. I am mentioning this here to caution those who want to pursue litigation. Everyone has a right to a fair and speedy trial by law. In my divorce case, the judge did everything she could to force a disposition. She interfered with due process, and did not allow a fair and speedy trial. When it became apparent that the custody case and relocation of my son was not going to settle, the judge took the following actions: First, she met with both parties and their attorneys, in a diner, completely off the record. She was trying to force a settlement. She also discussed her political views on the Middle East— again, inappropriate. Second, she said to me in court, "Don't you tell me how to parent a child; I am a divorced mother of two." This has no bearing on my case, and her ability or inability to parent properly should not have become an issue. Third, she told me, after she told the stenographer to stop typing in court, "If you try the case, I am going to let your ex-wife relocate with your son." I responded, "Go ahead and try the case." She manipulated the proceedings of the court to threaten and blackmail me, and she did not allow me a fair trial, which I was entitled to by law.

On the other hand, I have been in front of judges who understand what is happening very quickly, and can make decisions very quickly. They remain objective and listen closely to what both parties have to say. By listening, unbiased, they can make decisions that are fair, and more likely based on facts rather than prejudice or preconceived opinions.

Once again, the judge is another risk in litigation. You do not know if you are getting a good one who is fair and unbiased, or a bad one who manipulates the court proceedings and abuses his or her power. Once again, it is always better to stay out of court and negotiate a settlement.

Review of Chapter

Going to court and litigation is a very big deal. It can be scary and intimidating. It requires a lot of preparation and practice. It can be very costly and requires a great deal of legal hours. Once you go to court and start litigation, the results may be out of your hands. It will be up to a judge, or perhaps a jury, to make the decisions that will affect your life.

Always conduct yourself professionally and politely in the courtroom, no matter who it is you see, or how much you like or hate them.

There is an art to being examined and cross examined, and that needs to be practiced and perfected with your attorney. An attorney who does not properly prepare you for this is not a good attorney.

Judgers are the rulers in the courtroom. Like any other field, there are good judges and bad judges. The judge is a great risk when it comes to litigation, and a bad one can ruin people's lives. Always be aware of this when you are considering negotiation versus litigation.

Now that either a settlement has been negotiated or a judgement has been made and entered, let's look at the next chapter, which is what to do when it is all over.

Notes

83

Notes

84

Notes

85

Notes

CHAPTER 7

Step 7: Live with the Decision or Negotiation

Now that you have made it to this chapter, all the fighting, arguing, backstabbing, politics, negotiating, litigation, and rulings are now over. However, your life is not over. You probably have many years left. Assuming there are no appeals—that is another book—the case is done. You may have won big, or you may not have gotten what you wanted. Again, winning is really achieving what you decided was winning, back in chapter one. How close did you come? The odds are, if you negotiated, you are much closer to what you wanted than if you had gone to trial. Litigation through trial may be more interesting and exciting than negotiating; but you, hopefully, want the best outcome, not the most excitement. No matter what happened, you did the best you could, especially if you followed the tips, guidelines, and warnings in this book. If you didn't, well, I told you so.

If you were awarded money or property, make sure to pursue it, or have your attorney pursue it. Just because people agreed to part with their money or property, or were ordered to part with their money or property, does not mean that they want to. You may still need your attorney to collect the money.

A good example of this is when I had to pursue an attorney after the Bar Counsel awarded me $12,000. There was an attorney I fired because, after looking through my case, he had another attorney, who I never even met, look through my case, and he charged me double. When I received the bill, I had a panic attack. When I confronted my attorney about it, he used the same bullshit line that I have heard other attorneys use: "This is litigation; it's expensive." By the way, if your attorney ever says that to you, get rid of him/her immediately, and find someone else. Anyway, I was demanding my money back and, of course, he did not want to give it back. I went to the Bar Counsel; there was an arbitration hearing set, and I won $12,000. He even used that same stupid line during arbitration: "This is litigation; it's expensive." Anyway, after I was awarded that money, the lawyer, of course, did not want to pay me. So, I had to go back to the Bar Counsel, who then intervened, and I got paid immediately. It's funny, lawyers want to get paid right away. However, to get back from them what is rightfully yours, can be very difficult.

The lawyer, from whom I was awarded $30,000 in the botched case with the institution, is still paying me back monthly, and that was five years ago. I initially paid him a $25,000 retainer, immediately. Unfortunately, these are people we have to put our trust in. Anyway, the point is, if you are awarded money, pursue it by all means necessary, especially if it was from an attorney.

If you won custody of your children, or visitation, it is better to call it parenting time. No parent is a visitor to their child, and using the term *visitation* is degrading, unrealistic, and stupid. Then, by all means, follow the agreement or orders, and do what is best for your children. **Even the fact that the court system uses a term like *visitation*, is archaic and barbaric. Nobody visits their own child, ever.** This includes both parties, whether joint custody, sole custody, or non-custody. Remember: the court, a judge, or a so-called expert, never knows more about your own children than you do. Your child has probably suffered plenty through the process, and none of these alleged experts live with your children. Be aware of that, and do what is best for your children.

As time goes on, and the animosity of the court case gets further into the past, parents can adjust the rules to benefit their children and themselves. Children grow up. They become teenagers, and then adults. If you used your child as a weapon in the divorce or custody proceedings, it will bite you in the ass as they grow up. They will turn on you. This is something no lawyer is going to tell you. The lawyer just wants the money, and the judge most likely wants the case over. You still have the rest of your life to deal with your children, and your children's other parent.

If you did not win or get what you wanted, you can become depressed, and obsess about it. Don't let this happen. It is not worth it. You need to move on with your life. In a civil case, what you may lose is money, property, or rights with your children. Losing money and property does not feel good, but it will not kill you. Failure to win money, which may be considered losing, will not kill you either. If it doesn't kill you, it will make you stronger. Do not let a broken, unpredictable system ruin your life. If you lose rights or time with your children, although painful, it will change. Always remember that. Children grow up, and they are smart, and they know what is going on. I lost a lot of time with my son, yet he has been living with me for the past seven years. We are very close, and we even work together now. We are not only father and son, we are best friends. No matter how much others tried to hurt our relationship and keep us apart, it did not work. They failed and lost. In fact, at the writing of this book, my son just graduated college and is studying to take the LSATs to attend law school, and I run a very successful business. Our lives have skyrocketed, despite any past lawsuits or injustices committed to us.

Once the litigation is over, maintain your health. Continue to take care of yourself physically, emotionally, psychologically, spiritually, and financially. This can be a time to rebuild. If you lost money and feel broke, well, broke is just a circumstance that can change. Being poor is different, and a mindset that you don't want. After my divorce, I felt wiped out and broke. I was $106,000 in debt and had to pay child support and alimony. I thought I was finished. However, I developed my career and paid back all of the debt in two years. The divorce and lawsuits did not hold me back; they strengthened me to bounce back stronger than ever.

After my lawsuit with the institution, I lost 80% of my revenue, and went bankrupt. I bounced back with my own business and did not need to work for the institution anymore. I developed other skills and became a public speaker, author, coach, and entrepreneur. Those who tried to bring me down, failed. They did not win. I did. I wrote this book on how to win a lawsuit because, if you handle things right, and have the right perspective, then you win, no matter what. You can't lose. You can only win. Many times, losing is winning. What is definite is that losing is learning. Many people do not realize that. The most learning occurs when you lose—not when you win. No pain, no gain.

If the judge makes the decision in a civil case, then the odds are that neither side is going to get what they wanted. Be aware of this. Neither side may be happy. Again, it is all up to you and the context with which you view your situation. You only lose if you declare yourself a loser. Remember, you put in a lot of time and did the best you can. Some people do not like saying, *"You did the best you can."* They argue that this is like settling. Well, with lawsuits, that is exactly what you want to do. You want to settle. That is the best way to win. This is not the Superbowl or the World Series. There is no clear winner. You have done the best you can—be proud of yourself, and look at yourself as a winner. If you were sued, well, you ended the case; now, pick up the pieces and move on.

Finally, when it is all over, you should get a divorce. You may be thinking, *what is he talking about?* Divorce your attorney. Finish up with him/her; settle any financial issues, and divorce him/her. The less they are in your life, the better. After all, whenever you speak with them, it costs money. So, now is the time to stop paying them, and use your money for much bigger and better things. Of course, if you are friends with them, or are married to them, or there are attorneys in your family, well, they are people and loved ones, and you are not divorcing them. But you should divorce your own attorney, and end the relationship. At least until next time when he/she is absolutely needed.

91

Review of Chapter

When the lawsuit is over, you need to go on with your life. Pursue your rights and your winnings. If you were being sued, then be glad it is over, and do whatever you have to do to move on with your life.

You never really lose unless you tell yourself that you did. Learn from your experience. Rebuild your life if necessary, and maintain your health and well- being, no matter what.

Finally, divorce your attorney, and be glad it is over.

Notes

93

Notes

94

Notes

Notes

96

ABOUT THE AUTHOR

William Snow is an author, speaker, and entrepreneur. William Snow is the author's pen name. He uses a pen name so he can write his controversial books with more clarity, realism, and educational value, without the risk of a lawsuit. He is a college graduate with advanced education. He loves movies and television. He is talented in many fields, including writing and public speaking. He is a successful entrepreneur whose businesses retired him from working years ago. He loves to travel, attend personal development courses, and work out at the gym.

William Snow has one son and multiple pets.